The Savoy Kitchen

A family history of Cajun food

Sarah Savoy

KITCHEN PRESS

In loving memory of Myrtle Riley, "Mom" Mabel Savoy, Joel "Pop" Savoy, Mary "Queen of Food Porn" Herczog, Gil Young, Linus Bertrand, "Cinnamon Bun" Bill Shepherd, Christian Gualdi, and the fabulous Les Blank.

First published in Scotland by Kitchen Press
1 Windsor Place,
Dundee, DD2 1BG

Text copyright © Sarah Savoy
www.sarahsavoy.com

Illustrations copyright © Jen Collins
www.hellojenuine.com

Photography copyright © Gabrielle Savoy (www.gabriellesavoy.com), Nick Barber, Philip Gould (www.philipgould.com), Marsha Polier Grossman (www.morninggorystudio.com), Chris Strachwitz, Ann Savoy, Sarah Savoy, Tim Kness, Festival Cousins d'Amérique, Gloria Maso, Wilson Savoy, Manolo Gonzales, Daniel Dubois, Lucius Fontenot, Raleigh Powell, Martine Verbrugghe, Sarah Le Menestrel, Camellia Cosgray, Joby Catto.

Design and front cover photography by Anti Limited
www.anti-limited.com

All rights reserved. No part of this publication may be reproduced, stored in a retrieval system, or transmitted in any form or by any means, electronic, mechanical, photocopying or otherwise, without prior permission of the copyright owners.

A CIP catalogue record for this book is available from the British Library.

ISBN: 9780957037335

Printed and bound in Scotland by Bell & Bain Ltd.

Kitchen Press Ltd
www.kitchenpress.co.uk

Acknowledgements

Thank you for your support in having purchased this book. I sincerely hope that it will bring you many fun moments of cooking popular Louisiana dishes to please yourself, your family, and your friends. Remember to make many of your meals parties with music and good company, and let the good times roll!

If you have any questions or comments, please e-mail Kitchen Press (info@kitchenpress.co.uk) and they'll have a page on their website (www.kitchenpress.co.uk) for any amendments or reader feedback.

Thanks to everyone who has influenced me by serving me great food, taking me out for great food, talking and writing to me about great food, and thanks to family and friends who have left their marks in our family recipes. Thanks especially to Mom, Dad, Joel, Wilson, and Gabrielle, the five of whom have made me who I am, always encouraged and supported me, who are all hugely inspirational to me in so many ways, and who have been the kick-ass party at most of the best meals I've ever enjoyed. Special thanks to Mom for sharing the handwritten recipes and photos from my childhood, and to Gabrielle for the use of her gorgeous photos. Thanks to Mildred "Lalla" Robinson, Juanita "Tulie" Ardoin, Charles "Coonie" Ardoin, Claude and Linda Ouellette, Albert and Rose Rozas, Tina Pilione, Carl and Susan Brazell, Steve Hochman, Linzay Young, Dirk Hebert, Chef Pat Mould, Steve Riley, Chuck Taggart, Corinne Gonzales, Alain Del Sant, Anita Conrade, Margot Deschamps, Gerard Viel, François Louwagie, Katerina Bohmova, Thierry Lecoq, Percy Copely (for the regular dinner food porn photo competitions), Hassan Allen, and Doc and Viviane Martinet. Thanks to Graham and Angie Breakwell for all the cooking demos they've booked for me and for being a hugely-important vehicle for me making a name for myself. Thanks to Annie Menter and Roger de Wolf for really having set the cooking demo thing in motion by having us at WOMAD's excellent Taste the World. Thanks to Sara Le Menestrel for having gently reminded me each time we saw each other, "Have you been looking for a publisher for your cookbook, Sarah?" Thanks to Emily Dewhurst at Kitchen Press for having picked up my cookbook and for dealing with me so gently at one of the busiest times of my life. Thanks to Joby Catto for the beautiful artwork he did to promote the book and for the very personal, touching cover (and for the meat pies! Lord!). Thanks to copy-editors Camellia Cosgray and Hilary Scott-Buchanan who are magicians in my mind for having worked out all those crazy US-to-UK-to-EU conversions—y'all are rockstars!—and again to Camellia for also helping test the recipes. Thanks to Nick Barber for all his beautiful photos he's always shared, including the one on the book cover of me cooking. Thanks to Jen Collins for the fun illustrations in the book. And thanks also to Chefs Emeril Lagasse and John Folse for their inspiration to stay in the kitchen, which is one place I'm proud to say this woman is definitely happy to belong. I'm sure I'm forgetting to list lots of people, and I will bake y'all cookies if I forgot you.

Thanks also to David Rolland and Vincent Blin who have helped me so much in my cooking demonstrations (and concerts, and with babysitting, and finding gigs, and helping me many times in the kitchen, and always being willing to come over and eat when I call them at the last minute with "Help! I cooked too damned much food again!"); to my husband, Manolo Gonzales, for learning to eat all the spicy food I put on his plate; and to our daughter, Anna Marquette, for being such an enthusiastic Cajun-recipe guinea pig!

The publisher would also like to thank the many people who contributed and featured in the photos in this book. The contributors we could identify we have listed on the copyright page, but the images came from far and wide and were mostly from the Savoy family personal archive stretching back over the years so it's possible we haven't credited everyone. Please get in touch if you see a photo of yours in here and we'll add you to the list in the next edition! Featured in the photos are many people who are very dear to the Savoy family and have made impressions on Sarah's life including Linus Bertrand, Bill Shepherd, Albert Rozas and Claude Ouellette.

Contents

INTRODUCTION	P.6
NOTES	P.8
GLOSSARY	P.10
BREAKFASTS	P.16
APPETISERS	P.26
SALADS & SIDE DISHES	P.38
GUMBOS, BISQUES & SOUPS	P.56
MEAT & POULTRY	P.70
FISH & SEAFOOD	P.88
DESSERTS	P.114
INDEX	P.136

Introduction

Growing up in Louisiana, I developed a passion for food at a very young age. As early as preschool, I began inventing dishes that my very tolerant parents would allow me to cook. Unfortunately, I also had to try to eat them.

Food in Louisiana is almost always an affair. Families are generally large, and friends often gather for weekend lunches, special holiday meals, and dinners. Perhaps this is what drew me to food from the beginning. In Louisiana, a meal is never just something to eat, but rather a party: people talking and telling stories while preparing dishes, playing music while the food cooks, and then sitting down together to enjoy not only the meal but the company as well.

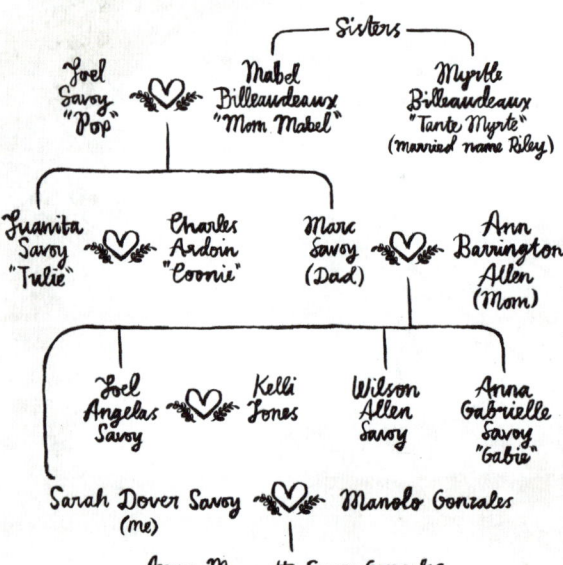

My family has been called "Cajun royalty." My father, Marc, is the man behind the **Acadian**, the instrument considered "the Rolls-Royce of Cajun accordions" by accordionists from many different genres of music. He opened his store up almost fifty years ago, and though most people said he'd never make it, he's one of the most internationally respected craftsmen and musicians in the world today. My mother, Ann, wrote the "bible" of Cajun music, **Cajun Music: A Reflection of a People**, and is still enjoying a career in music which has already spanned four decades. My brothers, Joel and Wilson, have several of their own bands as well, and Wilson won a Grammy for an album that Joel recorded on his **Valcour** record label. My sister, Gabrielle, is making a name for herself through her art and photography focused on Louisiana's people and events, and she is beginning to play music.

In my family's home, the kitchen has always been the centre of the action. It is in this room that Wilson was so often heard rocking the piano as early as six in the morning. Joel passed many an afternoon there playing beautiful jazz and Gypsy tunes on his fiddles and guitars, giving them all a Cajun flavour. Mom's favourite guitars stand near her rocking chair, waiting to be picked up late at night so Mom can play and sing her most-loved mournful ballads while the rest of the family is sleeping. Even today when we're all back home, Dad comes in from lacquering instruments in the backyard, picks up an accordion, tells my husband Manolo to grab a bass and starts playing – a loving smile on his face as he watches his granddaughter, Anna Marquette Savoy Gonzales, dance to the music.

The kitchen table was made by Dad himself and has seen just as many family games as it has meals. There'd always be children colouring on it and doing puzzles while the adults played music right behind them and a thick sauce simmered on the gas stovetop. I was always under foot when Mom and Dad were cooking. I wanted to chop vegetables, help put ingredients in the huge black pots, and watch my parents make my favourite dishes. Naturally I learned a lot from both of them and Cajun food is the one part of home I've been able to take with me anywhere I go. I spent five years living in Moscow, Russia and in the middle of the coldest winter – when the wind whistled through the old windows in my apartment and the white, weak sun shoved its way through thick grey clouds for only a few hours each day – I would often put on some Cajun music and start cooking a roux. Memories of cooking at home, laughing with my family, hit me with the heady aroma of the browning flour and gave me the sense that all was right with the world.

Cajun food is not the overblown, involved affair it is so often misconceived to be. New Orleans Creole food and Cajun food have little to nothing in common. Cajun food developed mainly out of necessity. When the Cajuns found themselves in Louisiana, they formed close communities. Mostly farmers, they grew rice and raised cattle, pigs and chickens, and the small, close-knit community would gather together to help kill the animals. Everyone ate and people took home meat to dry or smoke.

Cajun food is simple, filling, and pleasantly spicy. Because meat could not be kept very long without refrigeration, the spices were originally used to cover the flavour of meat that was beginning to taste less than fresh. Over time Cajuns developed a taste for the spiciness, but the "heat" of a dish should never cover the other flavours. Rather, to use my dad's analogy, "A good gumbo is like a good Cajun song. You hear everything that's going on. All the instruments complement each other and it all fits together to make one song." Extra cayenne, hot sauce, vinegar from pickled peppers, slivers of garlic shaved from the clove with a pocket knife, or even minced habañero peppers are added to the bowl at the table according to everyone's personal preferences.

When the idea of teaching Cajun cooking demonstrations first began to take shape, I found that I wanted to teach everything all at once. It was hard to choose which dishes were most important, which were most representative, even which ones were my favourites. I eventually decided just to put all my recipes in a book. For Christmas 2005, my mom, the queen of heartfelt gifts, gave me a handmade book of family recipes she had collected from my two grandmothers. Many of the recipes in this book are family recipes from my dad and his mom in which I've adjusted the ingredients to make cooking them outside of Louisiana possible, but most are my own creations or Louisiana favourites I have taught myself to make. These dishes are not the kind you'll find in restaurants, which are too often geared toward tourists, but rather the kind of food you'll find at someone's home when you're invited to dinner in Louisiana.

I have been pretty loose with the measurements for salt, pepper and cayenne because I really feel each cook add these to his or her own taste. If you want it my way, come find me and we'll cook something together. You'll also notice that these recipes are for serving a lot of people–that's just what I like to do. I hope you'll invite friends over to laugh and play music with you while you cook. If not, most of these dishes only get better as they sit in the refrigerator for a day or two. If you keep them any longer, then I haven't done a very good job of writing this book.

Bon appétit, y'all!

Sarah Savoy

INTRODUCTION

Notes

My dad was doing one of his cooking demonstrations somewhere on the east coast of America once and someone in the audience asked, "Do you not wash your rice?" When Dad told him we didn't, a woman next to him was overheard to mutter, "Wash their rice? They don't even wash their shrimp!" I'm sure in her mind we also grow up wrestling 'gators every afternoon after school. (What on earth was she doing at that demonstration anyway? I hope she learned something.)

No, we do not rinse our rice before cooking it. In Cajun dishes, the rice should stick together slightly in clumps to be broken up in individual bowls. (Please do not read that and go out and buy sushi rice, though, or something like that, as it's far too sticky.) Rinsing rice removes a lot of the starch that helps it to stick like that. If you live in an area where grains are often sold with pebbles and other debris mixed in, pick carefully through the rice before cooking it.

Always use long grain white rice. My parents have begun using brown rice in a few dishes like gumbo and it's very good; I've even made quinoa jambalaya! But to get started in Cajun cooking, let's do it the traditional way. I haven't yet found a store in Europe that sells Louisiana long grain rice, but I have had good luck using Thai long grain rice as a substitute. I cook it the same way, it tastes very similar to our rice back home, it looks almost the same, and it sticks together. Basmati can work too.

Cajuns are big fans of Hitachi rice cookers and one finds bragging rights in having the biggest one around! If you don't have one, cook the rice "the old-school way" like I do:

Pour the rice into a medium-sized heavy pot with a lid. Pour water into the pot to 2 centimetres over the top of the rice (Dad and I always measure this by placing the tip of an index finger on the top of the rice and filling the pot with water up to the first knuckle of that finger. We have big hands, though…). Salt the water and boil over high heat until the top of the rice is exposed – this can take anywhere from 5-12 minutes, depending on your stove and how much rice you're cooking. Cover the pot and immediately reduce the heat to the lowest possible. Steam for 17 minutes. At no point should you stir the rice; just let it cook. We do not add butter or oil.

When cooking recipes that call for fresh hot chilli peppers, please use caution. Wear rubber gloves if it's comfortable for you, or at least wash your hands very well after cutting the peppers, soak them in milk for 2 minutes, and wash them again. The acid in hot peppers can not only burn your fingers, but it also stays on your hands for hours (sometimes even a couple of days) after working with them. I don't know how many times I've touched one of my eyes hours after cutting up a jalapeño or chilli pepper and spent the rest of the day with a red, swollen eye.

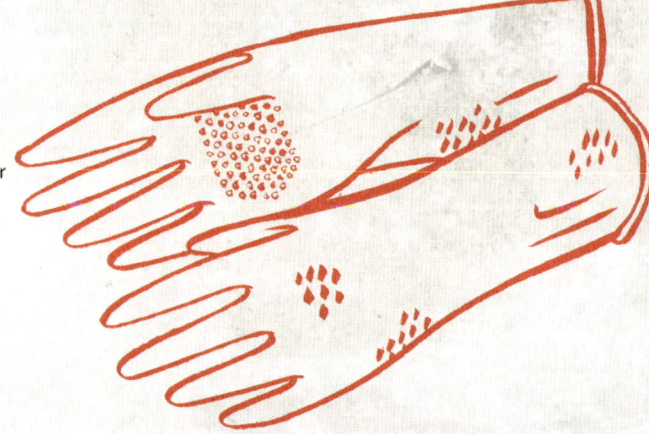

NOTES

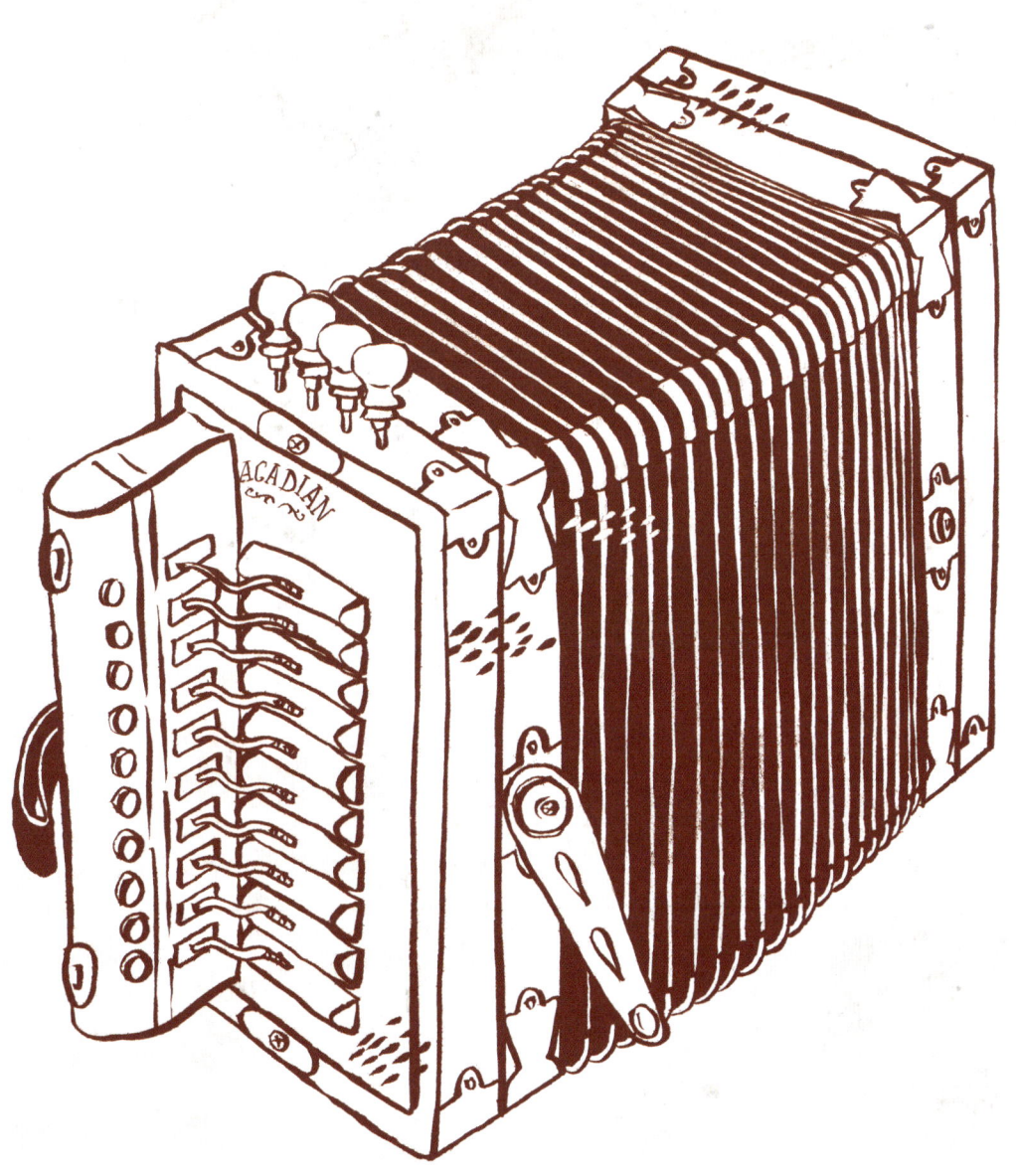

Glossary

After reading the first UK edit of this cookbook, I feel like I can now tell people I actually speak (or at least can read and write in) four languages: American, French, Russian, and Brit. I'm winking on that last word – y'all don't get mad.

The nice people at Kitchen Press thought it would be best if I added this glossary to make sure anglophones around the world know what I'm talking about in these recipes. At first I was surprised to see all these extra u's popped in all over the text, like "flavor" became "flavour" and "color" became "colour", but at least Mom is still herself and didn't become a mum or, worse yet, a gauze-wrapped mummy.

But let's get on with the major stuff here, and those of you in the US are going to need this glossary just as much as those of you in the UK!

Aubergine	is an eggplant, and if you speak French you already knew that one
Bicarbonate of soda	is the name baking soda uses to feel more interesting when she's hanging out in scientific circles
Caster sugar	caster will always make me think of castor, but this is just a finer ground white sugar, like superfine sugar. Wanna get confusing for a second? The French call this kind "sucre en poudre" and so of course you're gonna think about powdered sugar, right? Well, I am...
Crayfish	will work for those of you outside Dixie's Deep South, but back home we call them crawfish, like the title of Elvis' song in King Creole, and then again some people call them mud bugs or crawdads
Frying pan	is a skillet is a frying pan is a skillet. Ha! And they are the same thing, but when I think about a frying pan I picture a skimpy little thing coated in Teflon. When I think of a skillet I want an heirloom cast iron "black pot" skillet that smells faintly of past breakfast bacon, has a beautiful shine to it as it's perfectly seasoned by generations of use, and takes some muscle to pick up.
Grill	is not the barbecue but the broiler of your oven – that really hot part up top used for melting cheese over crab meat and stuff like that
Hob	is the stovetop, the burner, or the stove in general
Icing sugar	is powdered sugar or confectioner's sugar – what you'd use to dust over beignets or make buttercream icing
Lager	for those of you who class all beers as Budweiser and Coors or imports, lager is blond beer – like American beer – different from ale, white beer, heffeweise, stout, etc. We're just cooking with it, so pick up a PBR (that's Pabst Blue Ribbon for those of you outside of the Southern US, a beer that's sold in bars for a dollar) and run with it.

Mince	is not just a verb in this book, but is also ground meat, like for burgers or sausages (although sausages are really better when the meat is "minced" by hand, right? Right!).
Pastry	in my mind this should be an almond croissant, but in this book it's more specifically pie crust
Pepper	obviously you're going to find a lot of black pepper and cayenne pepper here, but when red or green peppers are mentioned, I'm talking about bell peppers, which some people also call sweet peppers
Pips	are not runty children or any relation to those brightly-coloured marshmallow chicks that freak me out around Easter time. In the UK, I learned just last night, pips are lemon seeds. So before you squeeze a lemon over that crab au gratin you've just cooked under your "grill," you might wanna remove the "pips."
Prawn	is what we call shrimp
Spring onions	are green onions in Louisiana, or sometimes scallions, and we mostly only use the green spiky tails
Tomato passata	When I was a kid I went through a phase where I only wanted to write the French spelling of my name, Savoie. Well, this is what tomato sauce calls herself when she wants to remind everyone of her Italian origins.
Vegetable shortening	is unavailable in France, though you can walk into almost any store and buy a jar of lard or rendered duck fat. What in the UK you may buy under the brand Trex, I import from the US in my suitcase as Crisco. I've learned to make most things without it, but there's still nothing better for frying chicken.

Now for those of you in the UK, there's some stuff you're not likely gonna know right off the bat, and other stuff you're gonna need explained a bit more than I can really do within each recipe. So…

Blue crab	We went through quite a bit of back and forth trying to figure out how crabs compare across the continents. The blue ones that we eat in Louisiana are smaller than the brown crabs I've found in Europe, their pincers are smaller and their bodies thinner, more angular and pointy at the sides. The brown ones, which the French call "torteau", are bigger and rounder, with swollen-looking pincers. But you know what? Those fat brown boys only have about half the meat that our blue crabs have! Since eating or cooking crab is already quite a bit of work, I prefer my efforts to be rewarded by huge chunks of white lump crab meat and I'm always disappointed by brown crabs. That said, if that's all you can get, it's still crab, and it still tastes great! For recipes that call for white lump crab meat, you may have to order it online. I do, as all I can find at the fishmonger's in France is a mix of white crab meat and brown. That works well for many dishes like a seafood gumbo or stuffed mushrooms, but for something finer like crab cakes, you really have to insist on white lump crab meat. You could also of course splurge on a king crab, but I'd better stop there before I get too excited.

GLOSSARY

Cra-y-fish	In the UK you can buy farmed Chinese crayfish in tubs or order whole crayfish from suppliers like Crayfish Bob. The crayfish we eat in Louisiana are the Procambarus clarkii species (usually called red freshwater crayfish, bayou crayfish, or Louisiana crayfish), which is probably what you'll get if you order Chinese crayfish. Crayfish Bob supplies signal crayfish, which look a little different, but are very close in taste. I've never eaten boiled signal crayfish, but in this book we're only using them in dishes with other ingredients so those will work perfectly well!
Creole seasoning	Yes, you're going to see this in a lot of recipes. Please, please, please do NOT go out and buy any kind of Cajun seasoning that you're going to find in Europe. There are several good brands in Louisiana that you can possibly find online, but better you go there yourself and load up like I do. My favourite is Tony's Chachere (pronounced SA-sha-ree), but some prefer Slap Ya Mama, which I know you can get at www.americansweets.co.uk and www.amazon.co.uk.
	I normally prefer to use my own mix when cooking unless I'm just seasoning meat before dropping it onto the barbecue grill, but Manolo and Anna Marquette and I put Tony's Chachere on our pasta, in our salads – just about everywhere – and I wouldn't feel like much of an authentic Cajun host if I didn't have some on the table when I have friends over for dinner. So you can make your own and keep it in an air-tight jar; just shake it up before you use it. Use it as a rub on meat or fish before cooking, to season a stew or soup, to add to your own plate at the table – wherever and however you'd like. When the dish is salty enough to your taste, it should be perfectly seasoned. You can tweak this very spicy recipe to suit your own tastes:
	4 tbsp sea salt
	3 tbsp cayenne pepper
	2 tbsp black pepper
	2 tbsp onion powder
	2 tbsp garlic powder
	2 tbsp paprika
	½ tsp dried thyme
	Cajun seasoning should NOT contain basil, saffron, curry, sesame, sugar or any other kind of pepper than black and cayenne… You might add a pinch of dried oregano to the mix but keep it simple.

GLOSSARY

Hot sauce	Tabasco, Louisiana, Crystal, Cajun Power, Slap Ya Mama and whatever other brands you can think of off the top of your head – they're pretty much all the same idea. Cayenne peppers and salt and vinegar. The only difference between brands is usually the ratio of pepper to vinegar. I'm a hot sauce freak – I'll drink a shot of hot sauce during a cooking demonstration to scare the audience and I like a burger dripping with it – but I don't put it in much of my cooking. I think it's again something that's more often added at the table than to the pot, but that depends on the dish. My personal favourite hot sauce is Crystal, but I've never found any in Europe. Tabasco is fine (and I love their jalapeño sauce, their habanero sauce and most of their other sauces other than the original); Louisiana is better – you use the one you prefer! Just be sure the peppers used are cayennes if you want authentic flavo-u-r – I love habanero hot sauce, and I use it when I find it, but original Louisiana hot sauce at its most basic is made with cayenne.
Pure cane syrup	Just seeing the yellow can of Steen's Cane Syrup (even a picture of it!) makes me want to bake. It's made by cooking sugar cane juice in open kettles until it condenses to create this delicious, thick, dark amber syrup. Pass me a tea cup of it with a slice of Evangeline Maid bread. Well, I'll stop drooling over my keyboard. If you can't find it, dark molasses works very well for most of the sweet recipes here.
Roux	There are a lot of "You might be a Cajun if…" jokes. Some of my favourites are "…you leave your coffee to cool and it turns to gel" or "…your wife greets you in the mornings with, 'Honey, I've got the rice cooking. What do you want for dinner?'" But the all-time greatest, if you ask me, is "You might be a Cajun if your child's favourite bedtime story starts with 'First you make a roux…'!" Roux, a cooked fat and flour mixture, is the base of many Cajun and Creole dishes and is the secret behind that smoky, rich flavour of Louisiana cuisine. In addition to the flavour, it is the main thickening agent in our sauces. You can't make a gumbo without a roux. A lot of people think we use tons of filé (ground sassafras leaves) in our gumbo, but if you know how to make a good roux, you don't need it. Filé should really only be used if you're crazy about the flavour of it, and then you should only sprinkle a little in your bowl. In our home, as well as in the homes of most Cajuns I know, we don't use it at all.
Sauce piquante	In French this just means "hot sauce", but in Louisiana it refers to a stew, usually tomato-based, always spicy, made with meat or fish, and served over rice. A "courtbouillon" is different because it's only ever made with fish, and very little liquid added means the sauce is actually a fish and vegetable stock. A gumbo is different because it's a soup. But there's really not much difference between an étouffée and a sauce piquante, other than the fact that, because a sauce piquante uses larger pieces of meat (or frog legs, alligator, whatever can be cooked a long time), it's going to have more sauce.

GLOSSARY

Smoked pork sausage	You might know this kind of sausage as andouille, which is something very different in France and Louisiana. When I talk about smoked pork sausage, I mean chopped pork meat, garlic, salt, black pepper, and cayenne stuffed into sausage casing and then smoked until it's cooked through and a dark red colour. If you go to Louisiana, make a pilgrimage out to LeJeune's Sausage Kitchen (Highway 13 heading from Eunice to Crowley) for the best smoked garlic pork sausage you will ever eat. I bring boxes of it back to France with me to keep in the freezer, using it sparingly to stretch it as far as possible. Just a few inches of one of these links used with other smoked sausage will make a gumbo taste just like it does back home. In France I use Montbéliard or the really cheap "saucisse fumé," but these always have a sweet undertaste that I find strange. Polish or German smoked sausages can also work. A lot of people substitute chorizo, but I find the Espelette pepper fights with the cayenne and just doesn't work with Cajun cooking.
Tasso	This makes for a delicious addition to almost any Louisiana dish. It's a chunk of pork shoulder that's been salt-cured, seasoned with cayenne and garlic, and hot smoked. It can be eaten on its own, cut into thin slices, or maybe served as part of a Cajun Eggs Benedict (like with a poached egg and a grilled slice of tomato on a polenta cake – y'all hungry yet?), but will lend tremendous flavour to your jambalaya or anywhere else you want to use it. Unfortunately, unless you're going to make your own, the closest you're going to get to authentic tasso in the UK is smoked bacon which really is so far off in flavour. I suggest you make your own: You need a 2.2kg/5lb chunk of pork shoulder about 10cm thick. Salt-cure it in 200g kosher salt, 70g sugar and 1 tsp curing or "pink" salt nitrite mix for 3 -4 hours. Dry it off, then rub with 4 tbsp cayenne and 1 tbsp each of black pepper, garlic powder and onion powder. Hot-smoke over apple wood – or any wood without too heavy a perfume – for 30 minutes or until cooked through. It keeps well in the fridge for a couple of weeks, or you can freeze it as soon as it's cool and just cut off frozen chunks when you need them.

I think that's about all for this crazy glossary, but I do have one more important note to make about the recipes in this book. Kitchen Press has worked very hard to convert all measurements and temperatures to make it easier for you to cook these dishes wherever you are, but you need to be sure you're not mixing and matching between UK and US quantities – pick one and stick to it!

GLOSSARY

Breakfasts

Couche-Couche	P.18
Beignets	P.19
Agnes' Biscuits	P.20
Flaky Biscuits	P.21
Pain Perdue	P.22
Crayfish Omelette	P.23
Sweet Potato Pancakes	P.24
Cajun-Style Breakfast Burritos	P.25

Couche-Couche

SERVES 4

My favourite mornings at home were when the cereal was left in its box on the shelf and Mom or Dad made breakfast. Mom did the best pancakes. Dad did hard-boiled eggs drizzled with vinegar and sprinkled with Creole seasoning. But the all-time favourite comfort breakfast was couche-couche. Dad would get out a huge, black, cast-iron skillet heavy enough to break my little arm, cook up the couche-couche, put a hot slice in a bowl, pour cold milk over it and sprinkle sugar on top. I also liked it with pure cane syrup. I never did get Dad to show me how he made it, so this is my own recipe and it does the trick for me.

```
3 TBSP VEGETABLE OIL
150G (1 CUP) YELLOW CORNMEAL
1/2 TSP BAKING POWDER
1/2 TSP SUGAR
1/2 TSP SALT
250ML (1 CUP) MILK

20CM CAST IRON FRYING PAN
```

Heat 2 tablespoons of oil in a frying pan with a lid over medium-high heat.

Mix the cornmeal, baking powder, sugar and salt in a large bowl, then whisk in the milk. Add the other tablespoon of oil.

Scrape the batter into the hot pan. Lower the heat to medium and cook, stirring regularly to avoid burning, for about 4 minutes. When the batter becomes thick, reduce the heat to medium-low, cover the pan tightly and cook for approximately 10 minutes until it forms a crumbly cake.

Remove the pan from the heat and let it sit, covered, for 10 minutes.

Cut the couche-couche into wedges and put one wedge in each bowl. Pour over cold milk or café au lait, mash it up and sprinkle with sugar or drizzle with honey, maple syrup or pure cane syrup.

BREAKFASTS

MAKES ABOUT 30

These were my brother Joel's favourites when we were kids. I remember he once burnt himself by dropping the dough in the hot oil. The splash of oil left a mysteriously quarter-note-shaped scar on his leg for a while. (Joel's just got that kind of crazy luck; he once found seven horseshoes walking home, has won every raffle he ever entered, and of course is an awesome awesome musician!)

These babies don't take much time or effort. Make the dough at least a few hours ahead (maybe more depending on how warm you keep your kitchen). This recipe makes about 30 beignets, but that's cool, because you can keep the dough in the fridge for at least 4–5 days, and you can also freeze it. If you want to freeze it, go ahead and roll the dough out once it's risen, cut it up, and freeze the dough shapes on wax or parchment paper until they're hard. Then you can put them in a freezer bag, take out as many as you want on any given morning, let them thaw an hour, and fry them up!

These are perfect with a big cup of hot coffee with milk or a black coffee flavoured with chicory in the style of Café du Monde.

1/2 TSP DRIED YEAST

75G (1/3 CUP) CASTER SUGAR

30G (2 TBSP) VEGETABLE SHORTENING (SUCH AS TREX)

1 LARGE EGG

4 TBSP DOUBLE CREAM

1/2 TSP SALT

450–600G (3–4 CUPS) PLAIN FLOUR

ICING SUGAR TO SERVE

VEGETABLE OIL FOR DEEP FRYING

Pour the yeast into a bowl or large mug. Add 4 tablespoons (¼ cup) of warm water and a tablespoon of the sugar, then stir the mixture with a fork until it's just combined. In another cup, melt the vegetable shortening in 125ml (½ cup) of hot water.

Meanwhile, gently beat the egg, cream, the rest of the sugar and the salt in a large bowl. Once the yeast mixture has started to froth, stir it in too, then add the melted shortening/hot water and mix well.

Add about 300g (2 cups) of flour and stir until it starts to come together pretty well. Then add another 150g of flour and knead the dough by hand until it is soft, elastic and not sticky. Only add the remaining flour if you need it to get a smooth dough.

Transfer the dough to a large bowl coated in a bit of vegetable oil, cover with a kitchen towel, and let it sit until the dough has at least doubled in size. (If you plan on making the beignets more than 4 hours later, let it rise in the refrigerator.)

Now for the fun part! Punch that dough ball down a few times, then roll it out on a floured surface until it's roughly 5mm thick. Cut the dough however you'd like. You can use cookie cutters if you want, but I prefer just cutting it with a very sharp knife into random squares and triangles (with sides of about 5 cm) and whatever other shapes happen. Set the pieces aside on wax paper or on the floured workspace so they don't stick together.

When you're ready to fry the beignets, heat a 1 cm depth of vegetable oil in a frying pan to hot but not smoking. Drop a piece of dough in to the oil to check the temperature – it should puff up right away and start turning golden after about 30 seconds. Fry the beignets in batches, taking care not to put too many in the pan. When they're golden on one side, turn them and let them brown a little on the other. You can keep turning them until they are golden brown all over. If they get dark too fast, you'll need to turn down the heat and remove the pan from the heat for a minute or two.

Set the fried beignets on a few layers of paper towels on a plate and sprinkle them with icing sugar. Let them cool for a couple of minutes before enjoying them with your café au lait (or chocolate milk).

BREAKFASTS

Agnes' Biscuits

MAKES 10

When my brothers and I were small, Dad would go to work and Mom would close herself upstairs to work on her book, *Cajun Music: A Reflection of a People*. We had a woman, Agnes, who would come over to cook, clean, and try to keep Joel and me outside where we couldn't do much damage to anything but each other. Wilson, just a baby at the time, got to stay inside in the air conditioning and smell the wonderful things she was always cooking – rice and gravy was one of my favourites, and we all loved her heart-stopping biscuits. This recipe is the closest I've gotten to recreating what she served us.

These are heavy biscuits, much more dense than the recipe for flaky biscuits that follows. They are great alone, filled with ham or cheese, spread with blackberry preserves, or broken into pieces and dipped in pure cane syrup. For dinner, try mixing in cheese, oregano and garlic (Joel's favourite); or any other flavours you'd like. Personally, my favourite way to eat them is using them to sop up a runny egg yolk.

```
220G (1 1/2 CUPS) PLAIN FLOUR
1/2 TSP BAKING POWDER
1 TSP SALT
125G (1/2 CUP & 1 TBSP) BUTTER, SOFTENED
125ML (1/2 CUP) BUTTERMILK, FRIDGE-COLD
30G (2 TBSP) BUTTER, MELTED
```

Preheat the oven to 220ºC (425ºF).

In a large bowl, sift the flour, baking powder and salt.

Cut the butter into the dry ingredients with two knives until only tiny pieces of butter remain. Add the buttermilk and stir just enough to combine, then turn it out onto a floured counter or work surface. Knead the dough very lightly until it's soft and not sticky.

Break the dough into 10 equal pieces and pat each down with your hand to a thickness of about 1cm. Place the biscuits, well spaced, on a lightly greased baking sheet.

Bake until golden brown (about 12 minutes), then brush each with a little melted butter while they're still warm.

BREAKFASTS

Flaky Biscuits

MAKES 10

So, there are biscuits for all kinds of people. I like 'em no matter how you serve them to me, as long as they're soft and just a little salty. I went nuts on biscuits when I first discovered buttermilk in France and, after about a week and a half of experimenting with ingredients and different pastry techniques, I landed on a very flaky biscuit that bakes up into layers and splits apart so perfectly to receive that pat of salt-crystal butter from Normandy... and they freeze beautifully! I manage about 10 biscuits with this recipe, so it's nice to double it and freeze the other half.

60G (4 TBSP) SALTED BUTTER, CHILLED

300G (2 CUPS) PLAIN FLOUR (GO FOR THE LIGHTEST GRADE FLOUR YOU CAN FIND)

1 TSP WHITE SUGAR

2 1/2 TSP BAKING POWDER

1/2 TSP BICARBONATE OF SODA

HEAPED 1/2 TSP SALT

250ML (1 CUP) BUTTERMILK, FRIDGE-COLD

Preheat the oven to 220°C /425°F.

First, cut the butter into very small cubes and put them on a plate in the freezer for 5-10 minutes.

Mix the flour, sugar, baking powder, bicarbonate of soda and salt together in a large bowl.

Using a pastry cutter or two knives, cut the very cold butter into the dry ingredients until you have coarse, sandy crumbs.

Stir in the buttermilk with a wooden spoon, but don't over mix. When the dough comes together, turn it out onto a floured workspace and knead it a little, then roll it out into a rectangle about 1cm thick. Fold the two short edges into the centre of the rectangle like a letter. Repeat this rolling and folding twice more (this is a pastry trick that forces the small chunks of butter remaining into layers within the dough, giving you that flaky texture once the biscuits are baked).

Use a 5cm diameter glass or biscuit cutter to cut rounds from the dough. Don't twist the cutter, as that seals the edges of the biscuit and prevents it from rising properly – just punch the cutter through the dough and set the biscuits, well spaced out, on a greased baking sheet. (If you want to freeze them, put the unbaked biscuits in the freezer on a piece of greaseproof paper, then transfer to a freezer bag once they are frozen solid.)

Bake for 10-12 minutes, until they are golden on top. Take them out of the oven, break them open and stick in a pat of butter, then serve immediately!

To cook frozen biscuits, put them on a greased baking tray without defrosting and put them into a cold oven. Turn the oven to 220ºC (425ºF) and bake for about 20 minutes – the biscuits will thaw as the oven heats.

BREAKFASTS

Pain Perdue

SERVES 5

I was thinking that maybe I shouldn't put this in a cookbook that I'm going to sell in France, but then I realised we might make this breakfast classic just a bit differently to the classic version. When I was a child, Louisiana didn't have the great bakeries that it does now, so we used slices of soft white bread instead of baguette. Mom could even sneak the "alien bread" (the heels of the loaves which Joel and I wouldn't touch) by us and we'd never notice, as long as it was covered in honey or syrup.

1/2 BAGUETTE (OR 10 SLICES OF WHITE BREAD)
500ML (2 CUPS) MILK
2 EGGS
2 TSP SUGAR
2 TSP VANILLA EXTRACT
2 TBSP BLACK COFFEE
DASH OF CINNAMON
DASH OF FINELY GRATED NUTMEG
30G (2 TBSP) BUTTER
2 TBSP VEGETABLE OIL
ICING SUGAR TO SERVE

Cut the bread diagonally into 10 slices, each about 1½ cm thick.

Mix the milk, eggs, sugar, vanilla, coffee, cinnamon and nutmeg in a large bowl. Put in the baguette slices and leave to soak until they are softened. If using soft, sliced bread instead of a baguette, just dip the slices into the milk mixture instead of soaking them, otherwise they'll fall apart.

Melt the butter in a large, heavy frying pan over medium heat, then add the oil. When it's hot, drop in 2 or 3 of the soaked bread slices at a time and cook them for 2-4 minutes per side until golden.

To serve, put two slices of fried bread on each plate. Sprinkle with icing sugar and drizzle with honey, maple syrup, or cane syrup.

Note: I've recently started dredging the soaked bread in finely chopped pecans before frying them. If you can find pecans that don't cost you your guitar, run with this!

BREAKFASTS

Crayfish Omelette

SERVES 2

This is one of my favourite Sunday brunches. Serve it with a garlic-packed green salad on the side!

If you're more concerned about presentation than I am, split the omelette recipe in half and make two separate ones. Just put the first one on a plate and cover it with another plate to keep it hot while you make the second one.

- 4 LARGE EGGS
- 3 TBSP MILK
- DASH OF HOT SAUCE
- 45G (3 TBSP) BUTTER
- 4 TBSP DOUBLE CREAM
- 15 CRAYFISH TAILS (OR 10 MEDIUM RAW PRAWNS)
- 2 SPRING ONIONS, FINELY CHOPPED
- SALT
- BLACK PEPPER
- CAYENNE

Whisk together the eggs, milk, hot sauce and a generous pinch of salt in a bowl. Set aside while you get on with the filling.

Melt 30g (2 tbsp) of the butter in a heavy frying pan over low heat. Add the cream and season with salt, black pepper and cayenne. Stir in the crayfish tails and continue cooking over a low heat until they are tender (about 8 minutes). Add the spring onions, then remove the pan from the heat.

In a large frying pan, melt the remaining butter over medium heat. Pour in the egg mixture and spread it evenly over the base by tilting the pan. Cook the omelette just until it begins to set and brown at the edges. Lower the heat and add the crayfish filling in a band across the middle of the omelette. When the top of the omelette seems set enough, fold the edges across the filling from each side, overlapping them.

Cut in half with a spatula and serve immediately.

BREAKFASTS

Sweet Potato Pancakes

SERVES 4

I had these one morning at a restaurant where a friend of mine was working. I don't remember the name of the place, but I do remember the pancakes – typical Sarah! It took some trial-and-error to make my own, but I'm very satisfied with the end result. I even found sweet potatoes in Moscow ("Imported from Louisiana"!) and made them for my friends – a big hit. Yeah, Russians are big fans of just about anything cooked as a blin (even calf liver or shredded courgette). You might never want regular pancakes again. Just a warning...

- 175G (6OZ) SWEET POTATOES
- 85G (HEAPED 1/2 CUP) PLAIN FLOUR
- 1 1/2 TSP BAKING POWDER
- 1/2 TSP SALT
- DASH OF CINNAMON
- DASH OF FINELY GRATED NUTMEG
- 1 EGG
- 180ML (1/2 CUP) MILK
- 30G (2 TBSP) BUTTER, MELTED

Bring a large pan of water to the boil and add the sweet potatoes whole, with the skins on. Boil them for about 30 minutes until they are tender. Shock them in cold, running water to loosen the skins, then peel them. Chop and mash the sweet potatoes to a thick purée and leave to cool.

Sift the flour, baking powder, salt, cinnamon and nutmeg together in a large bowl.

Beat the egg, milk and melted butter into the sweet potato purée, then fold the mixture into the dry ingredients until just combined.

Heat a lightly greased frying pan or griddle over medium-high heat. Pour in tablespoons of batter to make little pancakes, and cook until the surface begins to bubble and the edges set. Flip them over, and cook for another 1–2 minutes.

Serve with honey or sweet rhubarb preserves.

BREAKFASTS

Cajun-Style Breakfast Burritos

SERVES 4

Okay, so this is a more modern dish that must have come from Texas... or, um...McDonald's? I don't know. Anyway, it's really good and filling, but very rich. I call this sort a "lazy Sunday morning pyjama breakfast". Let everyone eat in their pyjamas, then get dressed and go out for a long walk through a field or something.

Friends have told me this is a great hangover cure. Personally, I go for a hot mug of gumbo broth on those mornings-after.

450G (1LB) COOKED CRAYFISH TAILS OR SMALL PRAWNS

60G (4 TBSP) BUTTER

1 MEDIUM YELLOW ONION, FINELY CHOPPED

1 GREEN PEPPER, FINELY CHOPPED

1 LARGE TOMATO, CHOPPED

4 LARGE EGGS

2 TBSP MILK

2 TBSP SOUR CREAM

70G (1/2 CUP) CHEDDAR OR MIMOLETTE CHEESE, GRATED

2 SPRING ONIONS, GREEN PARTS ONLY, CHOPPED

4 LARGE FLOUR TORTILLAS

SALT

BLACK PEPPER

CAYENNE

In a small bowl, season the crayfish with salt, black pepper and a pinch or two of cayenne to taste.

Melt the butter in a frying pan and gently cook the onion and green pepper until the onions are soft and translucent. Stir in the tomato and continue cooking for another couple of minutes. Add the eggs and the seasoned crayfish tails and cook, stirring regularly, for 3–5 minutes more, until the eggs begin to set. Remove from the heat.

Stir in the sour cream, cheese and spring onions. Divide the mixture evenly between the tortillas, roll 'em up and serve immediately with some sliced tomatoes on the side.

BREAKFASTS

Appetisers

Boudin & Boudin Balls	P.28
Crayfish Balls	P.30
Barbecue Prawns	P.31
Barbecue Crabs	P.32
Seafood Stuffed Mushrooms	P.33
Hot Wings	P.34
Mini Aubergine Pirogue	P.35
Prawn Dip	P.36
Crab-Stuffed Jalapeños	P.37

Boudin & Boudin Balls

I've put this recipe under appetisers because I don't know many people outside of Louisiana who like to eat spicy meat and rice for breakfast, but at least one morning a week in Louisiana we have boudin for breakfast. Bring a hot box of boudin to a Saturday morning jam session at the Savoy Music Center and you'll be king or queen for... well, the morning at least. And, fine, I'll admit it, dang it – one of the first things I do when I get to Eunice is go to Eunice Poultry, pick up a pound of boudin and eat it in the car while driving around listening to KBON.

A meat grinder with a sausage-stuffing attachment isn't something everyone always has on hand. David Rolland (a great friend who plays accordion in my Cajun band) actually bought one for the sole purpose of making boudin in Paris. He's done a good job finding all the ingredients and, quite a cook, has enjoyed experimenting with different vegetables and meat (rabbit boudin, duck boudin, and he always insists on adding some raw red bell pepper for colour). If you don't have the equipment, ask your local butcher if they'll stuff the boudin for you for the price of the casings – they usually have a day a week when they make sausages anyway.

Boudin balls are delicious anytime, and they're especially good when you're craving boudin and unable to find or make it. I walked around many a Louisiana music festival with a boudin ball in a greasy napkin.

This recipe makes an enormous quantity for parties but it does freeze. Please read through completely before getting started.

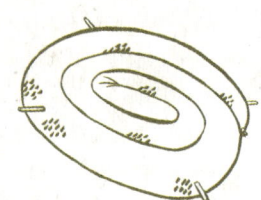

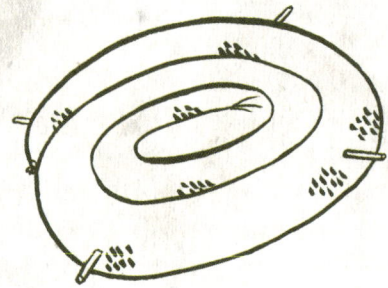

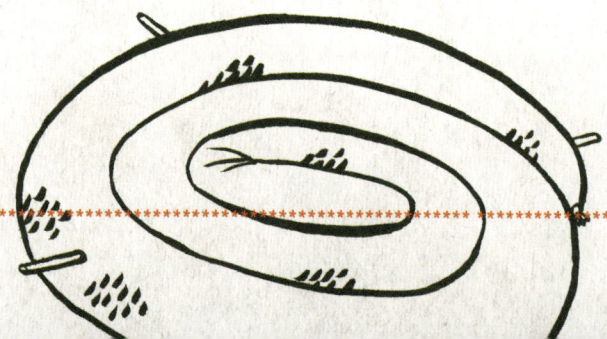

APPETISERS

Boudin

- 900G (2 LB) LEAN PORK MEAT
- 350G (3/4 LB) PORK LIVER (OR MIXED PORK AND POULTRY LIVER)
- 1/2 LARGE ONION, UNCHOPPED
- 1/2 RED PEPPER
- 1 GARLIC CLOVE
- 250G (1 1/4 CUPS) LONG GRAIN, WHITE RICE
- 1 LARGE ONION, CHOPPED
- 2 BUNCHES SPRING ONIONS, CHOPPED
- 1 BUNCH PARSLEY, CHOPPED
- SALT
- BLACK PEPPER
- CAYENNE

In a covered pot, simmer the pork meat and liver, the half onion, red pepper, and garlic in just enough water to cover. When the meat falls apart (after about an hour), remove it from the pot, discard the vegetables, and strain the broth.

Meanwhile, cook the rice as described on page 8, putting about 2 tablespoons of salt in the cooking water.

Put the cooked meat and chopped onion in a food processor or meat grinder with two thirds of the chopped spring onions and three quarters of the chopped parsley. Blitz or grind for a minute or two – you want to keep a bit of texture, so stop before it gets too smooth – then turn it out into a bowl. Stir in the remaining spring onions and parsley and the cooked rice, then slowly pour in enough of the reserved broth to make a moist stuffing. Season well with salt, black pepper and cayenne (about a ½ tablespoon each of salt and cayenne, and a teaspoon of black pepper), taste, and season again.

Use a sausage stuffer to put this into casings that have been soaked in cold water. Make long links not more than 45cm each, then tie off both ends, being careful to work out any air before you make the knot. Make a flat coil out of each link. Alternatively, ask your butcher to do it for you. You can freeze the uncooked links for several months.

To cook the boudin links, boil a large pot of water well seasoned with salt, black pepper and cayenne (or Creole seasoning, if you have it). Add a few links of boudin at a time then, once the water has returned to a gentle rolling boil, reduce the heat and simmer very gently for about 10 minutes. Be careful not to let them break.

Remove the boudin links from the hot water and set aside for at least 5 minutes, then cut them into equal 10cm sections to serve. Or, hell, just pass me the whole link.

This recipe makes a good kilo (2lb) of boudin. You can use any left-over stuffing to make boudin balls.

Boudin Balls

MAKES 20-25

- 450G (1LB) BOUDIN STUFFING
- 2 EGGS, LIGHTLY BEATEN
- 120G (2 CUPS) BREADCRUMBS OR CRUSHED CRACKERS
- VEGETABLE OIL FOR DEEP-FRYING

Using your hands, make golf ball-sized balls of the stuffing (or tennis ball-sized if you're gonna bring me some). Dip the balls in beaten egg, and then roll them in the breadcrumbs or crackers so they are fully coated. (You can freeze them at this point for up to a week.)

You can either deep fry or bake these. If you're frying them, pour vegetable oil to 5cm deep in a large pan and heat. Deep fry the balls until they're lightly browned all over, and drain on paper towels before serving. If you want to bake them, preheat the oven to 180°C (350°F) and put the balls on a baking tray. Bake for about 20 minutes, or until they're golden and heated through.

APPETISERS

Crayfish Balls

MAKES 20-25

- 450G (1LB) CRAYFISH TAILS
- 1/2 ONION, CHOPPED
- 1/2 RED PEPPER, CHOPPED
- 4 SLICES LEFTOVER WHITE BREAD, TORN INTO PIECES
- 1 EGG, BEATEN
- 1/2 BUNCH OF PARSLEY, CHOPPED
- 4 SPRING ONIONS, GREEN PARTS ONLY, CHOPPED
- 60G (1 CUP) BREADCRUMBS OR CRUSHED CRACKERS
- SALT
- BLACK PEPPER
- CAYENNE

- VEGETABLE OIL, IF DEEP FRYING

Using a food processor or meat grinder, process the crayfish tails, onion, red pepper and pieces of bread.

Add 2 tablespoons of water, the egg, parsley and spring onion tops. Mix it all thoroughly and season well with salt, black pepper and cayenne.

Shape the mixture into balls the size of golf balls and roll them in breadcrumbs or crushed crackers. If you're baking them, preheat the oven to 180°C (350°F). Put the crayfish balls on a lightly oiled baking tray in the oven for 20 minutes until golden brown.

If you'd rather fry them, heat vegetable oil to a depth of 5cm in a large, heavy pan. Fry the balls a few at a time until golden, then drain on paper towels.

APPETISERS

Barbecue Prawns

SERVES 4

I first had these at a restaurant in Basile, Louisiana, when my family and some of our friends went out for a fun dinner. The restaurant specialized in boiled crayfish, prawns and crabs, but the chef was also quickly gaining fame for Barbecue Prawns and Barbecue Crabs. No barbecue required, these prawns are baked in a spicy sauce. Peeling them is half the fun, but eating them and soaking up the juices with crusty slices of French bread seals the deal.

OLIVE OIL

900G (2LB) LARGE PRAWNS, UNPEELED, HEADS-ON

1 LEMON

150ML (2/3 CUP) BEER

1 TBSP WORCESTERSHIRE SAUCE

1 GARLIC CLOVE, MINCED

1 BAY LEAF

1/2 TSP PAPRIKA

1/2 TSP BLACK PEPPER

1/2 TSP SALT

1/2 TSP CAYENNE

90G (6 TBSP) BUTTER, CUT INTO CUBES

FRENCH BREAD FOR SERVING

Heat the grill to its highest setting.

Lightly oil a large baking tray and spread out the prawns in a single layer. Cut the lemon in half: cut one half into thin slices and squeeze the juice from the other half into a small bowl.

Add the beer, Worcestershire sauce, garlic, bay leaf, paprika, black pepper, salt and cayenne to the bowl of lemon juice and whisk until combined. Pour this over the prawns, then top them with the lemon slices and cubes of butter. Grill for about 6 minutes or until the prawns turn pink.

Transfer to a serving dish and serve with French bread for sopping up the juices. Great with a cold beer.

APPETISERS

Barbecue Crabs

SERVES 4

This recipe takes a bit more work than the Barbecue Prawns on the previous page, but it will be well worth the effort to any crab lover like myself. The blue crabs we get in Louisiana are much smaller than the brown crabs most commonly available in the UK, but have more meat in them – but you can go ahead and use brown crabs if that's all you can get.

- 4 LARGE BLUE CRABS, LIVE
- 3 GARLIC CLOVES, CRUSHED
- 2 TSP LEMON JUICE, FRESHLY SQUEEZED
- 1/2 TSP WORCESTERSHIRE SAUCE
- 1/2 TSP MUSTARD
- 1 TSP SALT
- 1 TSP CAYENNE
- 1/2 A LEMON, SLICED
- 90G (6 TBSP) BUTTER, CUBED
- CREOLE SEASONING (SEE P.12)
- VEGETABLE OIL FOR DEEP-FRYING

First, prepare the crabs as follows. Drop them into a clean sink full of iced water and let them sit for at least 8 minutes – this will stun them.

If you're using blue crabs: remove the main outer shell of each crab to kill it instantly. Use a knife to pry off the "key" (the spade-shaped piece of shell under the crab) and to remove the furry, spongy gills from each side of the body. Remove the crab's mouth parts by grasping them between two fingers and twisting. Rinse well. Break off the two big claws and set them aside. Break the body in half along the middle. Drop the crabs into a large pot of boiling water and boil for 3 minutes.

If you're using brown crabs, it's probably easier to boil the crabs before you cut them up – cook them for around 10 minutes, then twist off the leg and claws. Use your thumbs to push the softer core section away from the shell, then remove and discard the stomach and the pointed 'dead mans fingers' from the cavity. Chop the body in two.

In a small bowl, mix up the marinade: whisk 2 tablespoons of water with the chopped garlic, lemon juice, Worcestershire sauce, mustard, salt and cayenne.

Put the cooked crabs in a big bowl, then pour over the marinade while they're still hot. Mix them well and cover the bowl with cling film before placing it in the refrigerator to marinate for 2 hours. Toss the crabs in the marinade every 20 minutes to ensure that they are all marinating evenly and equally.

Heat the grill to its highest setting.

Put the crabs in a single layer in a large baking dish and top them with lemon slices and cubes of butter. Grill for 8-10 minutes until the crabs are red and sizzling. Sprinkle with Creole seasoning and serve very hot.

When each leg is twisted off, a large lump of meat should slide out with it. The bodies can then be broken up and the remaining meat dug out. The large claws can be cracked open with a lobster tool or nut cracker (or with the butt of a heavy knife, but watch your hands).

APPETISERS

Seafood Stuffed Mushrooms

SERVES 6

I first had something similar to these when working at **Catahoula's Restaurant** *in Grand Coteau, Louisiana. Grand Coteau is a beautiful little town between Opelousas and Lafayette and* **Catahoula's** *is one of the best restaurants in Acadiana. I never did get the recipe, but this is the closest I've come to recreating it.*

- 1 LARGE AUBERGINE
- 18 FRESH MUSHROOMS
- 60G (4 TBSP) BUTTER
- 100G (4OZ) CRAB MEAT
- 100G (4OZ) SMALL PRAWNS, CHOPPED
- 6 TBSP BREADCRUMBS
- 1 TBSP LEMON JUICE
- 2 TBSP SPRING ONIONS, GREEN PARTS ONLY, FINELY SLICED
- 4 TBSP (1/4 CUP) DRY WHITE WINE
- 100G (1 CUP) PARMESAN CHEESE, GRATED
- SALT
- BLACK PEPPER
- CAYENNE

Preheat the oven to 200°C (400°F). Cut the aubergine in half lengthwise, and place both halves flat side down on a lightly oiled baking tray. Roast for 30 minutes or until absolutely tender. Meanwhile, wipe the mushrooms clean, and remove and reserve the stems.

Scrape the pulp from the roasted aubergine and purée in a food processor. Add the mushroom stems and give another burst in the food processor to combine.

In a heavy based frying pan over medium-high heat, melt half of the butter. Add the aubergine and mushroom mixture and cook for 2 minutes, then stir in the crab meat and prawns. Cook for another minute then remove the pan from the heat. Stir in the breadcrumbs, lemon juice and spring onions. If the mixture looks too thick, loosen it with a tablespoon of cool water.

Stuff each mushroom cap with 1½–2 teaspoons of the stuffing.

Melt the remaining butter in a saucepan and whisk in the white wine. Drizzle this over the stuffed mushrooms, scatter with some grated Parmesan cheese and bake for 15 minutes or until they are heated through and the cheese begins to melt and brown.

APPETISERS

Hot Wings

SERVES 4-6

In all fairness, hot wings are probably American and not specifically Cajun, but I can't stop myself from including them because they sure make a great appetiser. Writing this book had me thinking so much about Super Bowl party food, barbecue food and party food in general – I didn't want to leave these guys out!

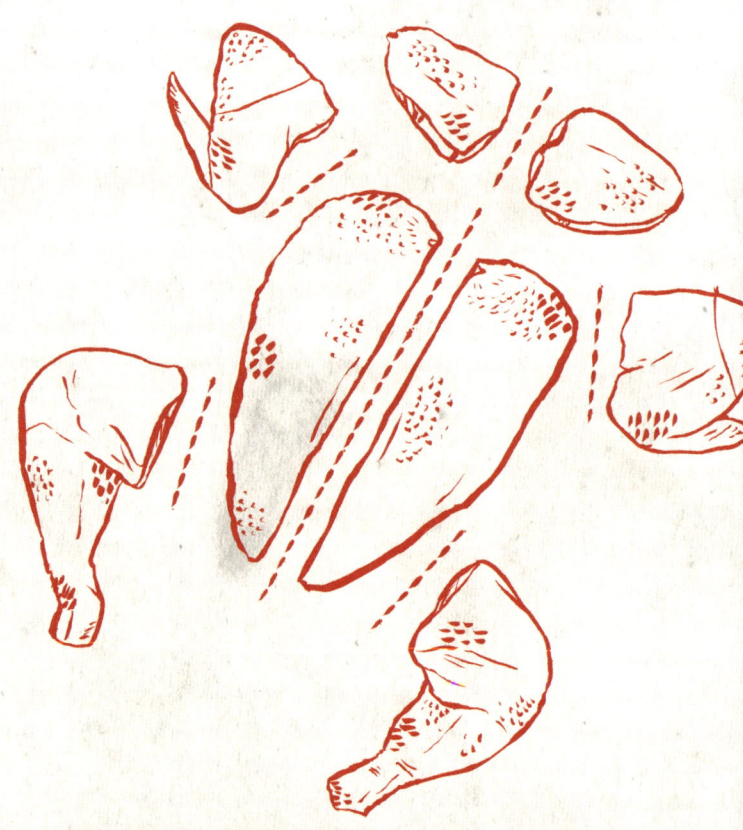

25-30 CHICKEN WINGS, CUT IN HALF AND WING TIPS SNIPPED OFF
185ML (3/4 CUP) BEER
2 GARLIC CLOVES, MINCED
40G (1/4 CUP) FLOUR
110G (1/2 CUP) BUTTER
5 TBSP HOT SAUCE
1/2 TSP FRESH THYME, FINELY CHOPPED
SALT
BLACK PEPPER
CAYENNE

VEGETABLE OIL FOR DEEP FRYING

Season the wings well with salt, black pepper and cayenne and marinate them overnight in the beer and garlic.

The next day, heat the vegetable oil in a large, deep pan or deep fryer. Drain the excess liquid from the wings, sprinkle over the flour and mix it all thoroughly. Deep fry the wings in small batches for about 10 minutes until they're golden brown and cooked through. Drain on paper towels and put them in a large bowl.

Melt the butter in a small saucepan over low heat. Add the hot sauce and thyme, simmer for 3 minutes, then pour over the wings. Mix everything up to be sure the wings are fully coated, then cover and leave to sit for 5 minutes. Serve warm.

I like to serve these with blue cheese dressing for dipping. Just whisk together:

250ML (1 CUP) MAYONNAISE
125ML (1/2 CUP) SOUR CREAM
90G (3OZ) CRUMBLED BLUE CHEESE
1 GARLIC CLOVE, MINCED
1 TBSP CIDER VINEGAR
2 TSP WORCESTERSHIRE SAUCE

Season with freshly ground black pepper.
You can keep this in a jar in the fridge for 3 days.

APPETISERS

Mini Aubergine Pirogue

SERVES 6

Tender miniature aubergines turn the classic aubergine pirogue into a fun appetiser, especially before Marc Savoy's Seafood Medley Courtbouillon or the Atchafalaya Special. These babies aren't very easy to find, so I'm always excited when I run across them.

- 12 MINIATURE AUBERGINES
- 2 TBSP OLIVE OIL
- 110G (4OZ) SMOKED SAUSAGE, CUT INTO VERY SMALL CUBES
- 1/2 SMALL ONION, FINELY CHOPPED
- 1/2 LARGE RED PEPPER, FINELY CHOPPED
- 2 GARLIC CLOVES, MINCED
- 60ML (1/4 CUP) DRY WHITE WINE
- 100G (4OZ) CRAB MEAT
- 100G (4OZ) SMALL RAW PRAWNS, PEELED
- 4 TBSP BREADCRUMBS
- 1 TSP FRESH PARSLEY, FINELY CHOPPED
- 2 SPRING ONIONS, SLICED
- 30G (2 TBSP) BUTTER, MELTED
- 2 TBSP LEMON JUICE
- 150G (1 1/2 CUPS) PARMESAN CHEESE, GRATED
- SALT
- BLACK PEPPER
- CAYENNE

Preheat the oven to 215°C (420°F).

Cut the aubergine in half lengthwise, then cut crosshatches into the fleshy side of each half. Bake them, cut side down on a lightly greased baking sheet, for 8 minutes. Turn them over and bake for 5 minutes more, or until they're tender. Leave to cool for 10 minutes, then scrape out the pulp and set it aside. Put the scraped out aubergine shells back on the baking sheet.

Reduce oven temperature to 180°C (350F).

Heat the olive oil in a large, nonstick skillet over medium heat. Add the sausage, onion, red pepper, and garlic. Sauté for 5 minutes. Add half of the reserved aubergine pulp and wine to the pan (you don't need the rest of the aubergine) and cook for 10 minutes, stirring regularly. Stir in the crab meat and prawns and cook for another minute. Remove from the heat. Add the breadcrumbs, parsley and spring onions to the aubergine mixture and season with salt, freshly ground black pepper and cayenne. Stir gently to combine.

Fill each aubergine shell with enough of the stuffing mixture to form a small mound (about 2–3 tablespoons). Whisk together the melted butter and lemon juice and drizzle it over stuffed aubergines, then top with Parmesan cheese.

Bake for 15 minutes or until the prawns are done and everything is hot.

APPETISERS

Prawn Dip

SERVES 6

- 225G (8OZ) COOKED PRAWNS, PEELED AND FINELY CHOPPED
- 110G (4OZ) CREAM CHEESE, AT ROOM TEMPERATURE
- 1 STALK OF CELERY, FINELY CHOPPED
- 1/2 ONION, FINELY CHOPPED
- 3 SPRING ONIONS, GREEN PART ONLY, FINELY CHOPPED
- 3 TBSP MAYONNAISE
- 2 TBSP FRESH LEMON JUICE
- 2 TSP WORCESTERSHIRE SAUCE
- DASH OF HOT SAUCE
- SALT
- BLACK PEPPER
- CAYENNE

Stir all the ingredients together in a large bowl. Transfer the dip to a pretty serving dish and chill in the fridge for at least 4 hours or overnight.

Serve with crackers, chips, and celery sticks for dipping.

APPETISERS

Crab-Stuffed Jalapeños

SERVES 4

These make a really fun spicy treat for an appetiser, or with a cold beer in the afternoon. I grow jalapeños on my balcony, but if you don't and you can't find them in the shops, pick a good-sized chilli pepper of your choice, heat-wise. Remember that the cream cheese in this recipe will cut back a bit on the heat of the pepper, so be a little daring! These are often prepared whole and then battered and fried, but this is the way I do it.

225G (8OZ) CREAM CHEESE, AT ROOM TEMPERATURE

225G (8OZ) CRAB MEAT (PREFERABLY LUMP MEAT, BROKEN APART WITH FINGERS)

3 SPRING ONIONS, GREEN PARTS ONLY, FINELY SLICED

1 GARLIC CLOVE, FINELY MINCED

8 LARGE JALAPENO PEPPERS (OR OTHER CHILLIS), SLICED IN HALF AND SEEDS REMOVED

30G (1/2 CUP) BREADCRUMBS

35G (1/4 CUP) CHEDDAR OR MIMOLETTE CHEESE, FINELY GRATED

SALT

BLACK PEPPER

Preheat the oven to 190°C (375°C).

Put the cream cheese in a bowl and beat it with a fork to soften it, then stir in the crab, spring onions and garlic. Season with salt and black pepper.

Stuff the mixture into the pepper halves until they're very full, then mix together the breadcrumbs and cheese and scatter over the top.

Arrange the stuffed peppers on a baking sheet and bake them for 30 minutes, or until the breadcrumbs are golden brown.

APPETISERS

Salads & Side Dishes

Potato Salad	P.40
Crayfish Salad	P.41
Spinach Salad	P.41
Ann Savoy's Southern-Style Coleslaw	P.42
Pops' Cabbage Salad	P.42
Corn Maque Choux	P.43
Smothered Okra	P.44
Creole Stuffed Tomatoes	P.45
Smothered Cabbage	P.46
Mexican Cornbread	P.47
Seafood Cornbread	P.48
Ann Savoy's Baked Beans	P.49
Onion Pie	P.50
Rice Dressing (Dirty Rice)	P.51
Oyster Dressing	P.52
Baked Sweet Potatoes	P.53
Zydeco Green Beans	P.54
Potato Grenades	P.55

Potato Salad

SERVES 6

My mom makes the best potato salad but I never learnt her recipe because she makes it different every time. Here's my own take – a little less heart-friendly!

Many Cajuns love to put a big scoop of potato salad right in their bowls with their gumbo. I really like it too, especially when I get a spoonful of hot gumbo with a bit of cold potato salad.

- 900G (2LB) NEW POTATOES
- 3 HARD-BOILED EGGS
- 120ML (1/2 CUP) MAYONNAISE
- 2 TBSP CHOPPED SWEET PICKLE
- 3 SLICES BACON, FRIED TO A CRISP AND BROKEN INTO SMALL PIECES
- 1 TSP CREOLE (OR WHOLEGRAIN) MUSTARD
- 1 RED ONION, FINELY CHOPPED
- 4 TBSP SOUR CREAM
- 1 SMALL BUNCH OF SPRING ONIONS, GREEN PARTS ONLY, SLICED
- SALT
- BLACK PEPPER
- CAYENNE

Boil the potatoes in plenty of salted water until tender, then drain, peel and chop into big pieces. Leave to cool.

Remove the yolks from the hard-boiled eggs and roughly chop the whites.

In a large serving bowl, mash the egg yolks in 2 tablespoons of the mayonnaise, then add the sweet pickle, bacon pieces and mustard. Gently stir in the potatoes, chopped egg whites and red onion, along with the rest of the mayonnaise and the sour cream. Mix it all well. Add the spring onion tops, then season the salad with salt, black pepper and cayenne and gently stir to combine.

Refrigerate until serving time.

MARC & ANN SAVOY
Photo: Chris Strachwitz

SALADS & SIDE DISHES

Crayfish Salad

SERVES 2

This is a good way to add a bit of Cajun flair to a dinner or lunch without going overboard on heavy rice or expensive seafood.

- 450G (1LB) COOKED CRAYFISH TAILS
- 1/2 ONION, FINELY CHOPPED
- 2 TBSP MAYONNAISE
- 1 TSP MILD MUSTARD
- 1 TBSP FLAT LEAF PARSLEY, FINELY CHOPPED
- 1/4 ICEBERG LETTUCE, SHREDDED
- 2 SPRING ONIONS, FINELY SLICED
- SALT
- BLACK PEPPER
- CAYENNE

Mix the crayfish tails, onion, mayonnaise, mustard and parsley together in a bowl and season with salt, freshly ground black pepper and cayenne.

Arrange some shredded lettuce on two small plates, then spoon half the crayfish mixture on top of each. Scatter with the spring onions and serve.

Spinach Salad

SERVES 4 (OR 6 AS AN APPETISER)

I first had this salad at a restaurant in New Orleans that offered a shrimp and oyster happy hour – $0.25 for either a raw oyster on the half shell or a boiled shrimp. It was that afternoon that I fell in love with the combination of spinach and oysters, whether raw or cooked. This salad is simple, and I doubt that it's unique to Louisiana, but I had to include it in this book to go with the oyster recipes in the Seafood and Fish section. You can also top this salad with some lightly-fried oysters for a pretty excellent lunch.

- 450G (1LB) FRESH BABY SPINACH, WASHED AND PATTED DRY
- 6 QUAIL EGGS, BOILED, PEELED AND HALVED
- 1 RED ONION, THINLY SLICED INTO RINGS
- 2 BIG HANDFULS OF SWEET CHERRY TOMATOES, HALVED
- 2 TBSP DIJON MUSTARD
- 3 TBSP HONEY
- 4 TBSP EXTRA VIRGIN OLIVE OIL
- SALT
- BLACK PEPPER

Arrange the baby spinach leaves on 4 plates and top each one with 3 halves of quail egg, a scattering of wafer thin onion rings and some halved cherry tomatoes. Whisk the mustard and honey in a small bowl with 1 tablespoon of water until well mixed. Season to taste with salt and black pepper, then keep on whisking as you slowly pour in the olive oil. Keep whisking until the dressing emulsifies.

Drizzle about 2 tablespoons of dressing onto each plate of salad and serve immediately.

SALADS & SIDE DISHES

Ann Savoy's Southern-Style Coleslaw

I love this stuff next to a hot barbecued chicken breast or even on a hot dog. (Yes, despite what my dad says on p.38, we do eat the occasional hot dog, especially on New Year's Eve as we sit on bales of hay around a huge bonfire in front of the barn, grilling hot dogs, drinking champagne and laughing.) My favourite picnic contribution is usually pulled-pork served on baguettes topped with this coleslaw.

450G (1LB) GREEN CABBAGE, GRATED OR FINELY CHOPPED
1/4 ONION, FINELY CHOPPED
2 CARROTS, GRATED
120ML (1/2 CUP) MAYONNAISE
4 TBSP MILK
1 TBSP CIDER VINEGAR
1/2 TSP SUGAR

Put the cabbage, onion and carrots in a large serving bowl.

Mix together the mayonnaise, milk, cider vinegar and sugar in a small bowl, then pour it over the cabbage and toss until everything is thoroughly combined.

Let the coleslaw sit for 5 minutes before serving.

Another of my favourite ways to prepare coleslaw is to slice the cabbage very finely, pour some salt over it, squeeze the salt through the cabbage to soften it a bit, then add the other ingredients above (along with a couple of cloves of grated garlic). My dad goes nuts for it this way.

Pop's Cabbage Salad

BOTH SERVE 6

225G (1/2 LB) BACON
450G (1LB) CABBAGE
1 TSP WHITE SUGAR
1 TSP WHITE VINEGAR
BLACK PEPPER

Fry the bacon in a pan until it's crispy.

Meanwhile, slice the cabbage into fine ribbons.

When the bacon is cooked, drain it on paper towels

Pour away most of the fat from the bacon pan, then whisk in the sugar and vinegar to the drippings and fat that is left. While this is still hot, pour it over the cabbage and mix well.

Chop the bacon and toss it into the salad with some freshly ground black pepper.

Yes, I love the Cajun idea of "eat your vegetables".

SALADS & SIDE DISHES

Corn Maque Choux

SERVES 4

Yum. The Cajuns learned to make this from their American Indian neighbours in Louisiana. This has been one of my favourite side dishes since I was very young. It's also excellent with crab meat (see the variation at the end of the recipe) and I often serve it that way as a bed for my crab cakes. Dare I admit that I've often made this with canned corn when fresh corn was unavailable? It's only a little different that way, but for the sake of authenticity, here is the recipe when using fresh corn on the cob. You'll figure out your own way of using canned corn if you want to.

5 EARS FRESH SWEETCORN, SHUCKED, SILK REMOVED
60G (4 TBSP) BUTTER
1 LARGE YELLOW ONION, CHOPPED
1/2 GREEN PEPPER, CHOPPED
2 LARGE TOMATOES, PEELED AND ROUGHLY CHOPPED
1/2 – 1 FRESH HOT PEPPER (CAYENNE OR GREEN CHILLI), SLICED (SEEDS REMOVED, IF YOU PREFER)
1 TBSP SUGAR
100ML (1/3 CUP PLUS 1 TBSP) MILK
SALT
BLACK PEPPER
CAYENNE

With a sharp knife, cut the corn from the cob in layers (whole kernels take too long to soften and this should be like a corn hash) into a large bowl. Scrape the knife along the empty cob over the bowl to collect any extra juice.

Melt the butter in a large, heavy skillet over medium-high heat, then sauté the onions, green pepper and tomatoes for about 7 minutes, or until the onions are translucent. Add the sliced hot pepper, corn and juice from the cobs, and the sugar. Season to taste with salt, freshly ground black pepper and cayenne. Cook, stirring frequently, for 15 minutes. Stir in 125ml (½ cup) of water and the milk, reduce the heat to medium and cook for another 15 minutes, or until the corn is tender.

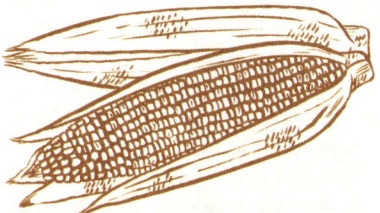

Crab Meat Variation

Prepare the corn as above. Sauté onion, pepper and tomato in half the butter, then proceed as above, replacing the milk and water with crab stock.

When the corn is tender, stir in the remaining butter a bit at a time, then add the spring onions and crab meat. Season to taste with salt, black pepper and cayenne. Remove from the heat and let it sit for 5 minutes before serving.

5 EARS FRESH SWEETCORN, SHUCKED, SILK REMOVED AND WASHED
60G (4 TBSP) BUTTER
1 LARGE YELLOW ONION, CHOPPED
1/2 GREEN PEPPER, CHOPPED
1 LARGE TOMATO, PEELED AND ROUGHLY CHOPPED
1/2 – 1 FRESH HOT PEPPER (CAYENNE OR GREEN CHILLI), SLICED (SEEDS REMOVED, IF YOU PREFER)
1 TBSP SUGAR
250ML (1 CUP) CRAB STOCK
3 SPRING ONIONS, GREEN PARTS ONLY, SLICED
125G (4 1/2 OZ) CRAB MEAT
SALT
BLACK PEPPER
CAYENNE

SALADS & SIDE DISHES

Smothered Okra

SERVES 6

When I was little, I used to cry when my dad would make me "at least taste" the smothered okra. These days, I could cry if I go too long without it.

- 450G (1LB) OKRA, WASHED WELL AND CUT IN 1 CM SLICES
- 110G (4OZ) SMOKED BACON, CUT INTO VERY SMALL CUBES
- 1 SMALL ONION, CHOPPED
- 1 GARLIC CLOVE, CHOPPED
- 3 TOMATOES, PEELED AND CHOPPED
- SALT
- BLACK PEPPER
- CAYENNE

Heat a heavy pot over medium heat. Put in the bacon and fry it in its own fat for 2 minutes. Add the onion and garlic and continue to cook for another 2 minutes, then stir in the sliced okra and cook until everything is well-reduced (about 20 minutes). Add the tomatoes and simmer for a further 10 minutes or until the okra is no longer slimy.

Option: According to your own taste, you may wish to add ¼ teaspoon of white vinegar, which helps to cut the viscous quality of the okra faster than cooking it for so long.

Also, because I like this so much, I often make it a main course by adding some sliced smoked pork sausage and more tomatoes, then serving it over steamed white rice with sliced tomatoes and cucumbers on the side.

It's also great with prawns, if you add them with the tomatoes and cook until they're steamed pink. You can also cook chicken thighs into it from the beginning. OR... you can make it completely vegetarian and it's still delicious.

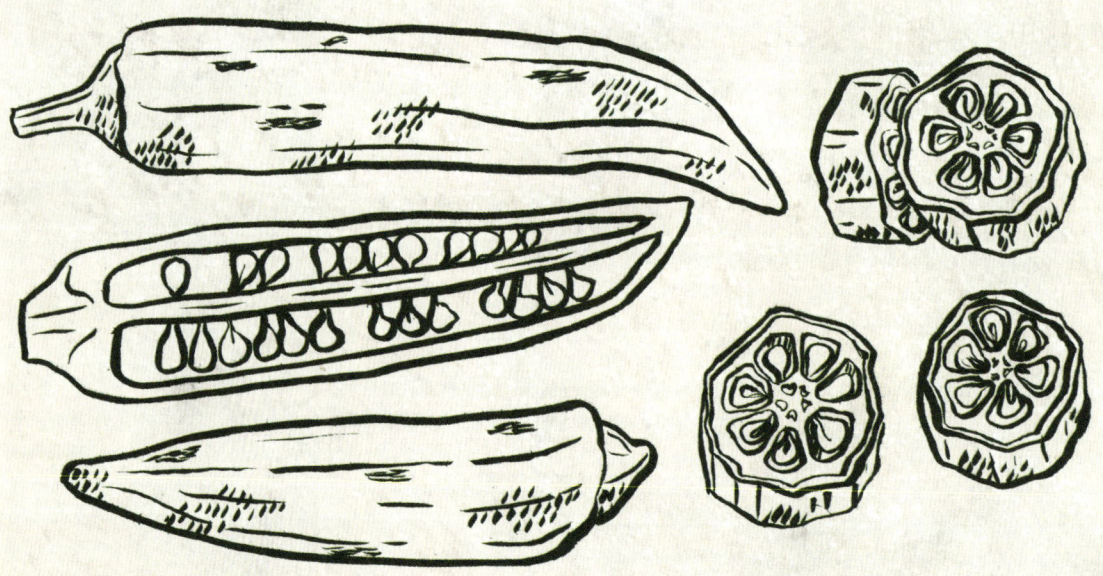

SALADS & SIDE DISHES

Creole Stuffed Tomatoes

SERVES 4

This recipe came about during a summer semester break from my university. Living in Lafayette in a rented house, I was daydreaming about having a little garden. I dug up a little rectangle of earth in the back yard, next to the parking lot, thinking that nothing would actually grow there. I planted 2 okra plants, 4 cucumber plants, and 6 tomato plants. Well, I don't know how it happened, but those cucumber and tomato plants produced more than I could ever possibly use. Four people were renting this house with me, and I quickly started coming up with as many ways as possible to use my home-grown produce. This is one of the recipes from that crazy culinary summer.

- 8 LARGE RIPE (BUT NOT SOFT) VINE TOMATOES
- 60G (4 TBSP) BUTTER
- 1 ONION, FINELY CHOPPED
- 1 GREEN PEPPER, FINELY CHOPPED
- 1 STALK CELERY, THINLY SLICED
- 4 GARLIC CLOVES, FINELY CHOPPED
- 225G (8OZ) SMOKED PORK SAUSAGE, DICED
- 10 SMALL PRAWNS, PEELED AND CHOPPED
- 1 TSP DRIED THYME (OR 3 SPRIGS FRESH)
- 2 TBSP FRESH PARSLEY, FINELY CHOPPED
- 150G (1 1/2 CUPS) LONG GRAIN WHITE RICE, STEAMED
- 140G (1 CUP) CHEDDAR OR MIMOLETTE CHEESE, GRATED (OPTIONAL)
- 2 TBSP BREADCRUMBS
- SALT
- BLACK PEPPER

Preheat the oven to 175°C (340°F).

Slice the top off each of the tomatoes and carefully scoop out the insides with a spoon. Set all the pulp aside in a bowl. Heat the butter in a large, heavy skillet over medium-high heat. Sauté the onion, pepper, celery and garlic for about 5 minutes, then add the sausage and cook for another 3 minutes. Stir in the prawns and continue cooking for 3 minutes, then add half the reserved tomato pulp, the thyme and parsley, and season the mixture to taste. Bring it to the boil and leave to bubble for a moment or two. Add a little more tomato pulp if it looks too dry, then remove from the heat and stir in the rice. Taste to see if the seasonings need to be adjusted.

Fill the tomatoes with the stuffing and place them in a baking dish. Top with the grated cheese, or put a little bit of butter on top of each one, and sprinkle with some breadcrumbs.

Bake the tomatoes for 20 minutes or until golden and bubbling. Serve immediately.

SALADS & SIDE DISHES

Smothered Cabbage

SERVES 4

I'll be honest. I still don't like the smell of cooking cabbage. In Russia, every apartment building I lived in smelt of it: I never did understand why. It's not like people can eat that much cabbage all the time, right? Anyway, the taste of smothered cabbage makes it one of the many dishes that excuses the smell. I love smothered cabbage. Lucky you if you have a black iron Dutch oven in which to cook it. (It's called a black pot in Louisiana and a lot of friends and relatives of mine made a festival named after it that quickly became one of the best in the state. Check out The Black Pot Festival.) Somehow, it always tastes best that way.

50G (2OZ) SMOKED BACON PIECES (OR THE SAME QUANTITY OF PICKLED PORK – SEE P.77)

50G (2OZ) SMOKED PORK SAUSAGE, CUT INTO 1/2 CM SLICES

1/2 ONION, CHOPPED

1 GARLIC CLOVE, FINELY CHOPPED

1 SMALL CARROT, GRATED (OPTIONAL)

450G (1LB) CABBAGE, CHOPPED INTO 3 CM SQUARES AND RINSED

1/2 TBSP BUTTER

SALT

BLACK PEPPER

CAYENNE

In a large, heavy pot with a lid, cook the bacon and sausage in their own fat over medium heat. Once they're browned and have released plenty of fat add the onion and garlic (and carrot, if using) and sweat for another 5 minutes. Pour about 70ml (just over ¼ cup) of cool water into the pot and scrape the bottom to deglaze it.

Pack the pot with as much of the cabbage as you can, put on the lid and reduce heat to medium-low. After 10 minutes, give it a stir and add any cabbage you couldn't fit in before. Season to taste, replace the lid and continue cooking, stirring every 10 minutes or so. When almost all the liquid is gone from the pot (about 20 minutes), add the butter and cook, covered, for another 5 minutes before serving.

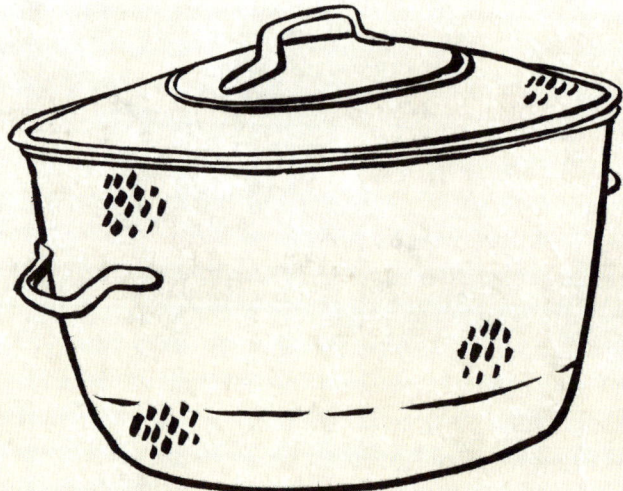

SALADS & SIDE DISHES

Mexican Cornbread

SERVES 8

This is a very popular accompaniment to just about all Cajun dishes. It's very good with barbecue, with pan-fried pork chops smothered in onions, with heated sausage links, and to sop up the gravy with any dish cooked in a sauce piquante. If you can find pickled jalapeño or chilli peppers, use a small can or jar instead of the one fresh pepper listed.

- 180G (1 1/4 CUPS) PLAIN FLOUR
- 160G (1 CUP) YELLOW CORNMEAL
- 1 TBSP SUGAR
- 1 TSP BAKING POWDER
- 1 TSP SALT
- 300ML (1 1/4 CUPS) MILK
- 125ML (1/2 CUP) VEGETABLE OIL
- 60G (4 TBSP) BUTTER, MELTED
- 200G (7OZ) TINNED SWEETCORN, DRAINED
- 2 LARGE EGGS, BEATEN
- 280G (2 CUPS) CHEDDAR OR MIMOLETTE CHEESE, GRATED
- 1 FRESH GREEN CHILLI PEPPER, SEEDS REMOVED AND THINLY SLICED
- PINCH OF CAYENNE

23 X 33CM BAKING DISH

Heat the oven to 180°C (350°F) and lightly grease your baking dish.

Sift together the flour, cornmeal, sugar, baking powder and salt. Stir in the milk, oil and melted butter. Quickly process half of the sweetcorn in a food processor, then add it to the batter along with the remaining whole kernels and the eggs, cheese, chilli and cayenne. Mix everything together really well and pour into the baking dish.

Bake the cornbread for 35–40 minutes until it is lightly browned and a toothpick inserted into the middle comes out clean.

Alternatively, you could make "Cajun Cornbread" like my Aunt Tulie and Uncle Coonie do.

Use the above recipe, changing out the chilli pepper for 450g (1lb) minced pork cooked with a chopped onion, 2 finely chopped stalks of celery, and 2 finely chopped cloves of garlic.

Add the cooked mince mixture at the same time as the corn, eggs & cheese etc, and bake as above.

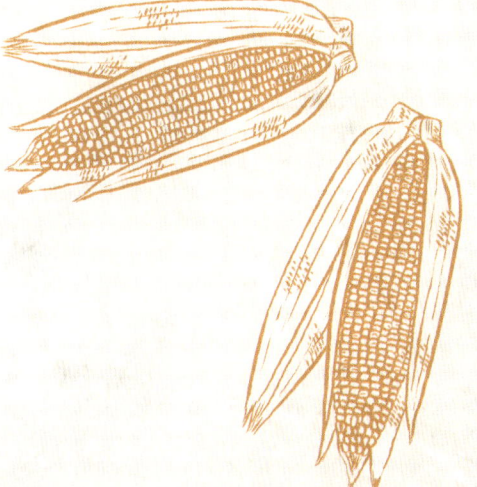

SALADS & SIDE DISHES

Seafood Cornbread

SERVES 10-12

This is one of my favourite things on earth. Yes, it's very rich and heavy. My mom won't even touch it because of that. But a friend used to bring it to me about once a month at my dad's shop on Saturday mornings and I guess I even preferred it to the hot boudin – not often I can say that!

- 160G (1 CUP) YELLOW CORNMEAL
- 150G (1 CUP) PLAIN FLOUR
- 1 TBSP SUGAR
- 3 TSP BAKING POWDER
- 1 TSP BICARBONATE OF SODA
- 250ML (1 CUP) MILK
- 2 EGGS
- 60ML (1/4 CUP) VEGETABLE OIL
- 150G (5OZ) COOKED CRAYFISH TAILS
- 150G (5OZ) CRAB MEAT
- 100G (3 1/2 OZ) SMALL PRAWNS
- 140G (1 CUP) CHEDDAR OR MIMOLETTE CHEESE, GRATED
- 1 ONION, FINELY CHOPPED
- 1/2 GREEN PEPPER, FINELY CHOPPED
- DASH OF HOT SAUCE
- SALT
- BLACK PEPPER
- CAYENNE

23 X 33CM BAKING DISH

Preheat oven to 190°C (375°F). Lightly grease your baking dish.

In a large bowl, sift together the cornmeal, flour, baking powder and bicarbonate of soda and season well with salt, black pepper and cayenne.

In another bowl, whisk together the milk, eggs and vegetable oil, then add the seafood, cheese, onion, green pepper and hot sauce. Stir this mixture into the dry ingredients until everything is well combined, then pour into your baking dish.

Bake for 45 minutes to an hour, until it is lightly browned and toothpick inserted into the centre comes out clean. Let sit the cornbread sit for 10 minutes before cutting it into squares and serving.

SALADS & SIDE DISHES

Ann Savoy's Baked Beans

SERVES 4-6

Yes! Put them next to the coleslaw and barbecued chicken and steak! Serve it all up with Mexican cornbread or hot, buttered biscuits! Have I mentioned we like to eat? And any meal is only better when Dad's cooking outside, Mom's bringing all her side dishes out to the table on the screen porch (avoiding the mosquitoes!), and we're all hanging around in the yard together. These baked beans are better than any I've tried anywhere. Lucky you if you have a slow cooker and get to walk away from them...

```
250G (1 1/4 CUPS) DRY CANNELLINI
OR WHITE NAVY BEANS
100G (4OZ) SMOKED BACON OR HAM
1/2 ONION, CHOPPED
60ML (1/4 CUP) MOLASSES OR
MAPLE SYRUP
60ML (1/4 CUP) TOMATO KETCHUP
1 TBSP MUSTARD
1 TSP SALT
1/2 TSP BLACK PEPPER
```

Put the beans in a large bowl and cover with cold water. Leave to soak overnight.

The next day, drain the beans and put in a large, heavy pot with a lid. Cover with at least 3cm of water and bring to the boil then simmer, covered, for 3 hours, stirring occasionally to ensure that they're not sticking to the bottom of the pot.

Remove a quarter of the beans to a heavy, heat safe bowl and process with a hand mixer for 10 seconds. Return them to the pot and add all the remaining ingredients. Cook the beans slowly for another 3 hours, stirring at least every 10 minutes.

(If you have a slow cooker, it's even easier. Just put the drained beans in with all the other ingredients, cover with water and cook on high for 4 hours.)

Transfer the whole lot to an ovenproof casserole or baking dish and bake at 170°C (325°F) for 40 minutes.

Did you run out to buy a slow-cooker halfway through reading this recipe?

SALADS & SIDE DISHES

Onion Pie

SERVES 6

I first had and fell in love with the pissaladiere at a party at the home of some friends just outside of Paris. Normally, this Niçoise dish is made with caramelised onions on a pizza-like base, topped with a lattice of anchovy fillets, and dotted with black olives. When I was raving about it to a friend of mine from New Orleans, he told me, "Well, honey, but Creoles make that too! You just don't find that old mess in the restaurants." What old mess? Apparently, this dish was originally created to stretch a small amount of meat to make a main course. I've combined the two very different onion pies to make my own.

FOR THE BASE (A STORE-BOUGHT PASTRY CASE WORKS JUST AS WELL)

- 1 TSP DRIED YEAST
- 225G (1 1/2 CUPS) STRONG BREAD FLOUR
- 2 TSP SUGAR
- 1 TSP SALT

FOR THE FILLING

- 45G (3 TBSP) BUTTER
- 3 LARGE ONIONS, THINLY SLICED
- 3 LARGE EGGS
- 250ML (1 CUP) SOUR CREAM
- 3 SLICES LEAN BACON
- SALT
- BLACK PEPPER

23CM HIGH-SIDED PIE PLATE

Stir the yeast into 125ml (½ cup) of warm water and leave it to foam up.

Sift the flour, sugar and salt into a large bowl. Make a well in the centre and pour in the foamy yeast mixture. Mix with your hands until a smooth dough comes together, then knead it on a lightly floured work surface until it's smooth and elastic. Put the dough in a clean, greased bowl, cover with a damp cloth and leave to rise in a warm place for 1–1½ hours, or until the dough has doubled in size.

Preheat the oven to 220°C (425°F). Punch it down and roll it out on a lightly floured surface to a circle big enough to line your pie plate. Push the dough carefully into the pie plate so you have a rim of about 4 or 5 cm and let it sit for 15 minutes to rise a little. Bake for 10 minutes, then remove from the oven.

Now for the filling. Melt the butter over low heat in a heavy frying pan. Add the sliced onions and cook with a pinch of salt until very soft but not brown. It can take up to 40 minutes for them to really cook down. Transfer to a mixing bowl.

Lightly beat the eggs, season with salt and pepper, and add to the onions. Mix them together gently. Add the sour cream and mix gently again, keeping the filling light and airy then pour it into the partially baked crust. Slice the bacon along its length into very thin strips and arrange them in a lattice pattern on the top of the pie.

Bake the pie at 200°C (400°F) for about 15 minutes until the bacon is crisp and the crust is lightly browned. Let it sit for 5 minutes before cutting into wedges and serving.

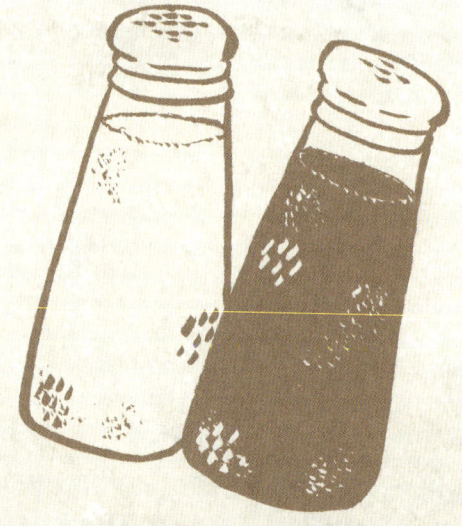

SALADS & SIDE DISHES

Rice Dressing (Dirty Rice)

SERVES 4

There are few occasions at my home for which Dad doesn't cook a rice dressing. Our normal Thanksgiving and Christmas menu is a huge green salad with lots of crushed garlic, baked turkey, rice dressing, candied sweet potatoes, and maybe a spinach and artichoke casserole brought over by Tina Pilione, family friend and Dad's assistant at Savoy Music Center. Dad raises chickens and turkeys. His turkeys are only fed corn, and are so big we normally have to cut one in half to fit it into the oven.

I probably shouldn't tell you that I used to make sandwiches from rice dressing as a kid – two slices of white bread filled with as much rice dressing as I could fit in. Carb special! Okay, and I still do it when there's leftover dressing in the refrigerator the day after Christmas, as long as no one's looking. I'm sure that plays no small part in the obscene amount of weight I gain every time I go home. This is my own recipe.

250G (1 1/4 CUPS) LONG GRAIN WHITE RICE

110G (4OZ) CHICKEN OR TURKEY GIBLETS

1 GREEN PEPPER, CHOPPED

225G (8OZ) LEAN MINCED BEEF

1 ONION, CHOPPED

1 SMALL BUNCH OF SPRING ONIONS, GREEN PARTS ONLY, SLICED

1 SMALL BUNCH OF PARSLEY, FINELY CHOPPED

SALT

CAYENNE

Cook the rice (see page 8 for how we do it).

Meanwhile, put the giblets and half the chopped green pepper in a pot with 250ml (1 cup) of water and bring to the boil. Simmer for 15 minutes over medium heat. Remove the giblets and roughly chop them (or grind them up in a food processor) then return them to the broth. If you chopped them by hand, you'll need to mash them into the broth with a fork.

In a large frying pan, brown the minced beef over a medium-high heat. Add the onions and remaining green pepper and cook for 8 minutes. Stir this into the giblets and broth.

In a large serving bowl, mix the cooked rice with the meat mixture. Season to taste with salt and cayenne, then gently stir in the spring onions and parsley. Serve hot.

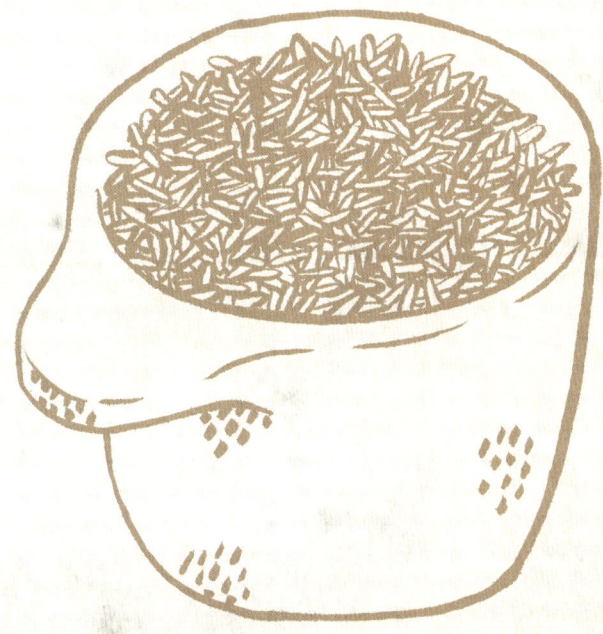

SALADS & SIDE DISHES

Oyster Dressing

SERVES 5

This is a special version of rice dressing that we sometimes have for Thanksgiving. It makes a delicious side dish with seafood, and it can also be stuffed into a chicken or duck before baking. Oyster dressing is Dad's favourite, and he makes it just the way his mom used to. This is my way.

- 200G (1 CUP) LONG GRAIN WHITE RICE
- 1 TBSP BUTTER
- 1/2 LARGE ONION, CHOPPED
- 1/2 GREEN PEPPER, CHOPPED
- 15 RAW OYSTERS, ROUGHLY CHOPPED
- 125ML (1/2 CUP) OYSTER LIQUOR
- 4 SPRING ONIONS, SLICED
- HANDFUL OF PARSLEY, FINELY CHOPPED
- SALT
- BLACK PEPPER
- CAYENNE

Cook the rice as usual (see page 8 for the way I do it).

Melt the butter in a large, heavy skillet over medium heat. Sauté the onion and green pepper for about 3 minutes or until they start to soften. Then add the chopped oysters and cook for another 3 minutes, stirring constantly. Season well with salt, black pepper and cayenne and remove the pan from the heat, then stir in the oyster liquor.

Mix the cooked rice with the oyster sauté in a large serving bowl. Stir in the spring onions and parsley, then cover the bowl and let it stand for 5 minutes for the flavours to blend. Check your seasoning before serving.

SALADS & SIDE DISHES

Baked Sweet Potatoes

SERVES 4

Let's hear it for Louisiana summers! It might get up to 42°C right around the time of my birthday every year (June 22), but that doesn't stop us from eating gumbo. What's the Savoy family's favourite way to eat gumbo? With a chilled, baked sweet potato right in the bowl! Maybe it's not too hot to have a huge pot of gumbo simmering away on the stove, but Mom did buy a convection oven so she could bake sweet potatoes out on the porch instead of heating up the kitchen any more than it had to be.

This is easy enough, but remember that sweet potatoes are…well, sweet! They contain a lot more sugar than regular potatoes, and those sugars can leak out while you're baking them and burn on the floor of your oven.

4 MEDIUM SWEET POTATOES

Preheat the oven to 200°C (400°F).

Wash the sweet potatoes. Leave the skin on and cut just the tips off either end.

Line a baking sheet with thick foil (less mess later means everyone's happy!), put the potatoes on it and pop it into the oven. Bake for 45-60 minutes or until they're very tender inside (check by pricking them with a fork).

Remove from the oven and let them cool, then refrigerate until serving time.

Sweet potatoes also make delicious fries: cut them into fries, toss in olive oil and some Creole seasoning, then bake at 200°C (400°F). You can also make crisps (or chips in the US): slice thinly, brush with olive oil and bake as above. Sprinkle with sugar and cinnamon for a sweet, healthy snack.

SALADS & SIDE DISHES

Zydeco Green Beans

SERVES 4

A popular expression in Louisiana used to be, "How are your string beans [haricots]?" You replied whether your beans were salty or not. If you were out of work, had the blues, were broken-hearted or hungover, your beans weren't salty. The song **Les Haricots Sont Pas Salés** ("The beans aren't salty") gave way to a whole style of music in Louisiana called Zydeco because of the way we run words together – while the French say "les 'aricots," in Louisiana we say "les-z-'aricots." So when you're listening to Zydeco, you're listening to string beans. Sounds good!

I'm just wondering how many afternoons I sat on the porch with my grandmother, or Agnes who came to clean and cook when we were kids, or Miss Lilian who used to babysit us, snapping the ends off green beans from the garden.

125ML 1/2 CUP) CIDER VINEGAR
225G (8OZ) GREEN BEANS
1/2 ONION, FINELY CHOPPED
1/2 TBSP SUGAR
1/2 TSP MUSTARD POWDER
2 GARLIC CLOVES, CRUSHED
1/2 TSP HOT SAUCE
200G (7OZ) STREAKY BACON (OPTIONAL)
SALT
BLACK PEPPER

Put the vinegar in a pot with 375ml (1½ cups) water, then simmer gently for 5 minutes. Put in the green beans and boil until they are tender but still bright green.

Let the beans cool in the liquid, then transfer everything to a large container. Stir in the onion, sugar, mustard powder, crushed garlic, hot sauce, a teaspoon of salt and plenty of black pepper. Refrigerate the beans overnight.

The next day, grill the bacon (if you're using it) until it's crispy, crumble it up and then scatter on top of the beans.

SALADS & SIDE DISHES

Potato Grenades

SERVES 4-6

```
6 LARGE POTATOES
15G (1 TBSP) BUTTER
1 ONION, FINELY CHOPPED
2-3 GARLIC CLOVES, FINELY CHOPPED
225G (8OZ) MINCED BEEF
1 EGG
1 TSP VEGETABLE OIL
DASH OF WORCESTERSHIRE SAUCE
SALT
BLACK PEPPER
CAYENNE
```

Peel the potatoes and use a small, sharp knife to make a tunnel (at least 2-3cm in diameter) from end to end of each one. Finely chop all the bits you've removed and set them aside.

Melt the butter in a skillet and sauté the onions and chopped potato together for 5 minutes. Add the garlic and cook for another 3 minutes, then stir in the minced beef and season well with salt, black pepper and cayenne. Cook everything for 8 minutes more, or until the beef is cooked through and the potatoes and onions are tender. Scrape it out into a bowl and leave to cool.

Once the meat mixture is cool, stir the egg into it, and then stuff into the potatoes until they're very full. When you've done them all, add a little bit of oil to the skillet and put in the potatoes. Season them well and brown lightly all over. Pour in enough water to come half way up the potatoes and add a dash of Worcestershire sauce and ½ teaspoon of salt. Then simmer gently for about an hour, turning occasionally to make sure the potatoes are cooking all around. They're done when they are very tender but not falling apart.

These make a great meal when served with a side of smothered okra (see page 44).

SALADS & SIDE DISHES

Gumbos, Bisques & Soups

Roux	P.58
Chicken and Sausage Gumbo	P.59
Seafood Gumbo	P.60
Prawn and Okra Gumbo	P.61
Green Gumbo	P.62
Crayfish Bisque	P.64
Crab and Sweet Potato Bisque	P.66
Turtle Soup	P.67
Navy Bean Soup	P.68

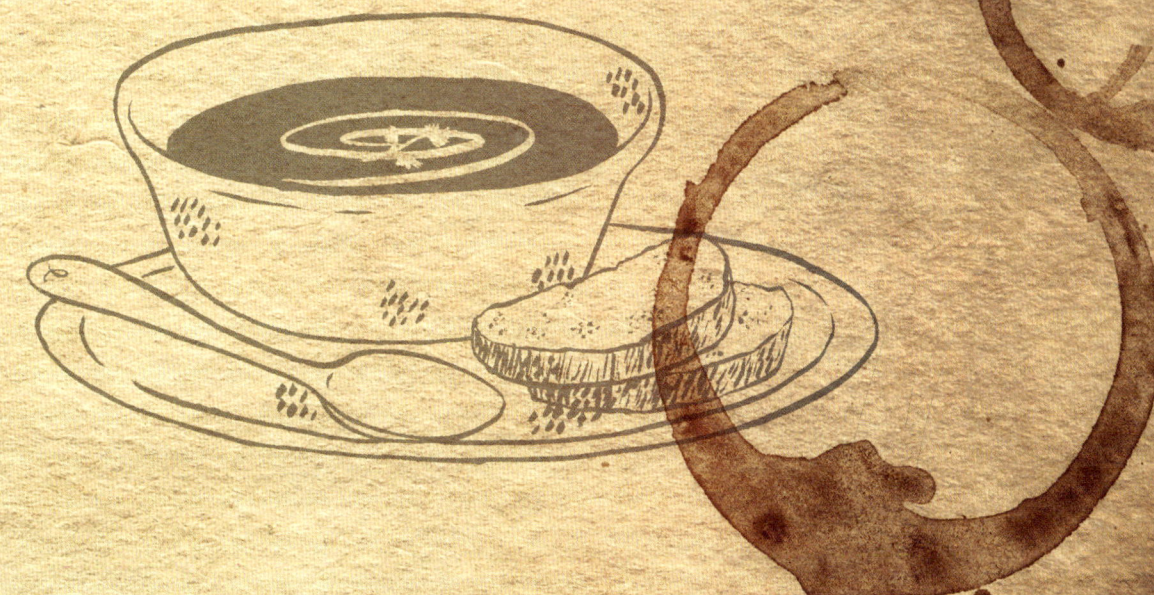

Roux

Roux is available in many stores in Louisiana. My dad used to make his own, but now, because it's easier and quicker, he keeps our pantry stocked with Savoie's Dark Roux in a jar (no relation to our family). In those rare moments I can find the time and patience (and energy in my arms), I make my own. Notice I have not written that I "like" to make my own. I can't think of many things I dislike doing more than making roux. It stinks up the house and it takes forever. Because of that, I always make it in huge quantities and keep it for up to two months in the fridge. I imagine there's a "zen of the art of making roux" that can be achieved with time. You'll understand what I mean when you start making this. For now, let me just advise you to open a window, feed the dog, and set your voicemail to pick up immediately – you're going to be stove-side for quite a while, and if you blink you'll burn your roux.

The kind of oil you use is very important. I once tried it with olive oil: it was very difficult to keep it from burning, and then it didn't even taste good. Peanut oil is gaining popularity in Louisiana as it seems to withstand the heat better than any other.

The quantities here will give you enough roux to make a gumbo with a little left over, so you might want to double it up and keep some in the fridge.

```
YOU WILL NEED:
250G (1 2/3 CUPS) WHITE FLOUR
350ML (1 1/2 CUPS) PEANUT OR
VEGETABLE OIL
```

Heat the oil in a heavy frying pan over medium-high heat. Get the oil pretty hot, then mix in the flour and stir manically until it's well-blended. Keep the heat on medium-high, and keep stirring. The roux is ready when it is a deep, dark chocolate-to-coffee shade of brown. The length of time this takes will vary depending on the type of pot you are using and the type and level of heat under your pot, but it can take anything from 30 minutes to an hour. Once the colour's right, allow the roux to cool almost to room temperature.

It is important to know that in a heavy cast iron frying pan, the roux will continue to darken once you have removed it from the flame. It's also good to know that roux gets really really hot when it's cooking, so take care not to splash it.

You can either use the roux immediately, or put it in a jar and keep it in the refrigerator. Pour off any oil that's gathered on the top before you use it.

GUMBOS, BISQUES & SOUPS

Chicken and Sausage Gumbo

SERVES 10

This is a favourite at the Savoy home. Summers are really too hot to want warm soup for dinner, but my dad doesn't care. He makes this year round. For me, it's comfort food: I can make it anywhere, and no matter how homesick I'm feeling, nothing will cure me better than the smell of gumbo cooking on the stove while I'm listening to a disc of Savoy-Doucet, the Savoy Family, the Pine Leaf Boys or the Magnolia Sisters.

This is also a dish that's fun to cook outside. If you have a very large pot, invite a lot of friends over for your Cajun feast. Sit around and drink beer, play music and laugh while your gumbo is cooking, then serve it with ice-cold beer or soda.

A note on ingredients: you can add whatever meat you like to a gumbo. The most common is this combination of chicken and sausage, but I have enjoyed rabbit gumbo, duck gumbo, squirrel gumbo, and so on. Dad makes a delicious turkey gumbo when he kills one of his turkeys. The tender breast meat holds together better than chicken but falls apart in your bowl. I've also heard of people using nutria and raccoons, although I've never tried either. Another favourite twist of mine is to crack whole eggs into the gumbo as it's cooking, about 5 minutes before adding the parsley and spring onions. There are as many gumbo recipes as there are triangle players, so you'll figure out your own favourite recipe. Cajun food is all about "taste and adjust", as family friend Gil Young always said.

My dad always uses garlic pork sausage from LeJeune's Sausage Kitchen in Eunice and all who have tried it will argue that it is the best. Stop by on your trip to Eunice and treat yourself to a 10–20 pound box. If you're in the UK or Europe, however, Polish smoked sausage like Kielbasa or Torunska will do fine, and in France I often use Montbéliard, but I prefer to slice and fry it first, both to cook out some of the fat and to give it a smokier flavour through browning it in a skillet. Use a big, fat, free-range chicken, weighing at least 1.5kg (3¼lb). You could joint it before cooking, but, personally, I do not care to have a whole piece of chicken sitting in my bowl of gumbo, so I cook it whole then shred the meat and return it to the pot.

- 250ML (1 CUP) ROUX (SEE P. 58)
- 1 LARGE CHICKEN
- 900G (2 LB) SMOKED PORK SAUSAGE
- 3 LARGE ONIONS, CHOPPED
- 2 LARGE GREEN PEPPERS, CHOPPED
- 1 SMALL BUNCH OF SPRING ONIONS, GREEN PARTS ONLY, SLICED
- 1 SMALL BUNCH OF FLAT-LEAF PARSLEY, CHOPPED
- SALT
- BLACK PEPPER
- CAYENNE

In a very large pot, bring 1 litre (4 cups) of water to a slow simmer. Add the roux and stir steadily until all the roux has dissolved and the mixture begins to foam up. Continue stirring while you add all remaining ingredients except spring onions and parsley. Then pour in another 2 litres (8 cups) of water so that everything is just covered.

The gumbo should simmer very gently over medium heat until the chicken is tender (about 45 minutes). Do not cover the pot and do not allow the gumbo to boil as this will break the thickening property of the roux.

Once the chicken is cooked, remove it and leave until it's cool enough to handle (if you're using chicken pieces, ignore this step.) Take off and throw away the skin, then pull all the meat off the bones. Put the shredded meat back in the pot and discard the bones. Add the spring onions and parsley and cook the gumbo for 15 minutes, then take the pot off the heat and let it sit for another 5 minutes. Using a shallow serving spoon, remove the fat and excess oil from the surface of the gumbo (Dad usually goes so far as to follow this step with an application of paper towels to the surface of the gumbo to ensure that all excess fat is removed).

Serve over steamed white rice. We like to add a chilled baked sweet potato or a scoop of cold potato salad to our bowl. Others like to add crushed saltine crackers.

GUMBOS, BISQUES & SOUPS

Seafood Gumbo

SERVES 8

Fresh seafood makes this dish perfect, but off-season it can be very expensive, even in Louisiana where the Gulf of Mexico provides the surrounding states with loads of fresh seafood year-round. Frozen seafood works just as well, though, provided you have the prawn heads and shells to make the stock. What we call "crab fingers" are the meaty part of the claw on the moveable part of the shell, with the rest of the shell cracked away..

- 500G (1LB) LARGE PRAWNS, UNPEELED
- 1 LARGE ONION, WHOLE
- 10 BLACK PEPPERCORNS
- 250ML (1 CUP) ROUX (SEE P.58)
- 2 LARGE ONIONS, FINELY CHOPPED
- 1 LARGE GREEN PEPPER, CHOPPED
- 2 GARLIC CLOVES, FINELY CHOPPED
- 225G (8OZ) RAW OYSTERS, SHUCKED
- 225G (8OZ) CRAB FINGERS
- 225G (8OZ) LARGE SCALLOPS
- 225G (8OZ) LUMP CRAB MEAT
- 1 SMALL BUNCH OF SPRING ONIONS, SLICED
- 1 SMALL BUNCH OF FLAT LEAF PARSLEY, CHOPPED
- SALT
- BLACK PEPPER
- CAYENNE

Peel and devein the prawns, keeping the shells and heads aside.

In a very large pot, bring 2 litres (8 cups) of water to a gentle boil. Add the prawn shells and heads, the whole onion and the peppercorns and simmer, covered, for at least an hour. Strain the stock and discard the prawn peelings, onion and peppercorns.

Return the stock to the pot and bring it back to a gentle boil. Reduce the heat to medium and add the roux, stirring steadily until all of the roux has dissolved and the mixture begins to foam up. Pour in a further litre (4 cups) of water, stir and season to taste with salt, black pepper and cayenne. Add the chopped onions, green pepper and garlic and simmer gently for 10 minutes (remember, don't let the gumbo boil or the roux will break).

Add the peeled prawns, oysters and crab fingers and simmer for 5 minutes. Next, stir in the scallops and crab meat and cook for another 5 minutes. Finally, add the spring onions and parsley and cook for a further 5 minutes. Taste for seasonings and adjust if you need to, then remove the pot from the heat and let it sit for 5 minutes more.

Serve over steamed, long grain white rice.

GUMBOS, BISQUES & SOUPS

Prawn and Okra Gumbo

SERVES 8

This is my mom's favourite gumbo, perhaps because it's lighter than the chicken and sausage version.

900G (2LB) LARGE PRAWNS, UNPEELED

250ML (1 CUP) ROUX (SEE P.58)

900G (2LB) MEDIUM-SMALL OKRA, SLICED CROSSWISE

3 LARGE ONIONS, FINELY CHOPPED

1 LARGE GREEN PEPPER, CHOPPED

3 CLOVES GARLIC, MINCED

1 TSP DISTILLED WHITE VINEGAR

1 SMALL BUNCH SPRING ONIONS, SLICED

1 SMALL BUNCH PARSLEY, CHOPPED

SALT

BLACK PEPPER

CAYENNE

Peel and de-vein the prawns, setting the shells and heads aside. Put all the peelings into a medium pot and cover with 2l (8 cups) of water. Bring to a boil then reduce the heat to medium and simmer for an hour, skimming the surface of the broth from time to time to keep it clear. Strain the stock through a wire mesh strainer, and discard the prawn shells & heads.

In a very large pot, bring the strained prawn stock to a gentle boil. Reduce heat to medium and add the roux, stirring steadily until all the roux has dispersed and the mixture begins to foam up. Stir in another litre (4 cups) of water and season to taste with salt, black pepper, and cayenne. Add the chopped onions, green pepper and garlic and simmer for 10 minutes, then throw in the okra and cook slowly for another 15 minutes, stirring frequently. Put in a teaspoon of vinegar, then gently stir in the prawns and simmer the gumbo until they are all pink and cooked through (15 minutes should do it). Finally, add the spring onions and parsley, taste for seasoning, and simmer for another 5 minutes.

Remove the pot from the heat and leave to sit for 5 minutes, then serve over steamed, long grain white rice.

GUMBOS, BISQUES & SOUPS

Green Gumbo

SERVES 10

This may well be the only really almost-vegetarian dish in all Louisiana cooking, but I have yet to prepare it for my vegetarian cousin, Emily. She, however, loves gumbo so much that she'll often have a bowl of broth and rice without the meat and just feel bad about it later.

Traditionally, Green Gumbo, or Gumbo des Herbes, was served during Lent when the many Catholics in Louisiana had to abstain from meat and seafood both. These days, most people just eat fish and seafood when they fast and abstain only from red and white meat. This gumbo has also all but vanished from our culinary culture.

The greens should really be just a mix of whatever you can find. I'll list the most practical ones, but I've also heard of carrot tops and turnip greens being used. I don't see why not.

1.35KG (3LB) GREENS INCLUDING SOME OR ALL OF THE FOLLOWING:
- 1 BUNCH OF SPINACH
- 1 GREEN OF CABBAGE
- 1 BUNCH OF COLLARD AND/OR MUSTARD GREENS
- 1 BUNCH OF CELERY TOPS
- 1 BUNCH OF WATERCRESS
- 1 BUNCH OF ROCKET

2 BUNCHES PARSLEY (1 FOR BOILING WITH THE OTHER GREENS, 1 SLICED & SET ASIDE)

1 LARGE WHITE ONION

1 GREEN PEPPER

3 STALKS OF CELERY, SLICED

2 GARLIC CLOVES, FINELY CHOPPED

150G (5OZ) SMOKED BACON, DICED (OPTIONAL)

250ML (1 CUP) ROUX (SEE P.58)

10 EGGS (OPTIONAL)

SALT

BLACK PEPPER

CAYENNE

Wash all the greens and 1 bunch of the parsley, and remove any tough parts like stems and/or veins. Put them in a large stockpot, cover with 3 litres (12 cups) of water and add a teaspoon of salt. Bring the pot to the boil, then simmer for 1–1½ hours until all the greens are really falling apart.

Meanwhile, sauté the onion, green pepper, celery and garlic for 10 minutes or until softened. (If you're using the bacon, sauté it with the vegetables as well).

Strain the greens over a bowl, then roughly chop them and return to the pot. Pour in the reserved stock and bring the pot back to a gentle simmer. Add the roux, stirring all the while until it dissolves, then stir in the sautéed vegetables and season to taste with salt, black pepper and cayenne.

Simmer the gumbo over medium-low heat for 40 minutes, being careful not to boil it. Crack the eggs into the pot (if you're using them) and scatter over the sliced spring onions and chopped parsley. Cook, covered, for another 10 minutes or until the eggs are set.

Serve over steamed, long grain white rice.

GUMBOS, BISQUES & SOUPS

Notice

Don't Fuck with my gumbo!

— Marc Savoy

Don't add anything, don't stir, Don't taste it, don't even get too close,...

Crayfish Bisque

SERVES 5

I want to be straightforward about this dish right from the start. It is difficult and time-consuming to make. It takes a lot of love, and a lot of standing over the kitchen counter, and it can hurt your fingers if you don't do it all carefully. However, it is good enough to, as we say in Louisiana, "make you wanna slap ya mama". I first had it at a restaurant in Eunice when my Great Aunt Myrtle Riley (Tante Myrt) took me out to dinner for my 7th birthday. I've had crayfish bisque a few times since, but nothing will ever top that first time I tried it. I've actually dreamed about that bisque and woken up to mutter bad language upon the discovery that it was only a dream. I kid you not.

To save yourself a bit of time and backache I suggest you boil the live crayfish and stuff their shells one day, then make the bisque the next.

- 5 TBSP CAYENNE
- 5 TBSP SALT
- 2 1/2 TBSP BLACK PEPPER
- 2 ONIONS, WHOLE
- 1 HEAD OF GARLIC, WHOLE
- 2 LEMONS, HALVED
- 1 1/2 TBSP MUSTARD SEED
- 2 TBSP THYME LEAVES
- 3 BAY LEAVES
- 1 1/2 TSP WORCESTERSHIRE SAUCE
- 5KG (11LB) CRAYFISH, LIVE

To cook the crayfish

Fill a very large stockpot with 6 litres (1½ gallons) of water and add all the ingredients except the crayfish. Bring the pot to a rapid boil and let it bubble over a medium heat for 15–20 minutes until the water is well-infused with the seasonings.

Quickly, tip in the live crayfish and boil them for 8 minutes. Then remove the pot from the heat immediately and drop in at least one large tray of ice cubes. Let the crayfish sit in the cold water for at least 15–20 minutes.

When the crayfish are cold, drain them and discard the stock. Break off the crayfish tails and carefully peel them, discarding the vein. Place the peeled tails in a bowl along with the yellow fat from the tail-end of the shell and mix it all well.

Prepare 30 of the shells for stuffing. Use the handle of a spoon to remove all the inside parts (including the eyes and antennae) until all that is left resembles a taco shell.

- 1 MEDIUM ONION
- 1/2 GREEN PEPPER
- 3 TBSP PARSLEY, CHOPPED
- 4 SPRING ONIONS, SLICED
- 90ML (6 TBSP) PEANUT OIL
- 130G (2/3 CUP & 2 TBSP) FLOUR
- 1/2 SEAFOOD BOUILLON CUBE DISSOLVED IN 6 TBSP HOT WATER
- 75G (1 1/4 CUP) FRESH BREADCRUMBS
- 1 EGG, BEATEN
- 30G (2 TBSP) BUTTER
- SALT
- BLACK PEPPER
- CAYENNE

For the stuffing

In a food processor, blitz the onion, green pepper, parsley and spring onions to a rough paste.

Heat 2 tablespoons of oil in a large pan, then stir in 2 tablespoons of flour and cook it until you have a blond roux (the colour of peanut butter). Remove from the heat and add the onion paste, taking care not to get burned by sputtering oil. Stir in half of the crayfish tail/fat mixture from earlier, and cook it for 10 minutes. Off the heat, mix in the bouillon, breadcrumbs, egg and butter to make a thick, sturdy stuffing that holds together well. Season to taste with black pepper and cayenne and add a splash more water if it's too dry, or more breadcrumbs if it's not thick enough.

Fill the empty crayfish shells with the stuffing, and keep any left over to add to the bisque later.

Heat the remaining oil in a large frying pan. Roll each stuffed shell in flour and then fry them until the stuffing is golden brown. Drain on paper towels. At this point the shells can be placed on a tray and refrigerated until the next day.

GUMBOS, BISQUES & SOUPS

45G (3 TBSP) BUTTER

60ML (1/4 CUP) PEANUT OIL

55G (1/3 CUP) PLAIN FLOUR

1 LARGE ONION, FINELY CHOPPED

1/2 GREEN PEPPER, FINELY CHOPPED

2 GARLIC CLOVES, FINELY CHOPPED

2 SPRIGS FRESH THYME
(OR 1 TSP DRIED)

1 SMALL BUNCH OF SPRING ONIONS, GREEN PARTS ONLY, FINELY SLICED

30 STUFFED CRAYFISH SHELLS

SALT

BLACK PEPPER

CAYENNE

For the bisque

Melt the butter in a heavy frying pan over medium heat, then add the peanut oil and flour and keep stirring until you have a light-brown roux. Off the heat, carefully stir in the onion, green pepper and garlic, then return to the hob and cook until the vegetables have softened.

Meanwhile, bring 2 litres (8 cups) of water to a gentle boil in a large stockpot. Stir in the vegetable/roux mixture and continue stirring until any lumps of roux have dispersed. Add the remaining crayfish tails and fat, as well as any unused stuffing, and turn the heat down to low. Season to taste with salt, black pepper and cayenne and simmer for 15 minutes.

Gently put in the stuffed, fried crayfish shells and simmer for 25 minutes, then add the spring onions and simmer for 5 minutes more.

Serve the bisque in soup plates, dividing the stuffed shells evenly between them. Eating the stuffing out of crayfish tails takes a bit of practice if you want to be delicate about it. I suggest using a fork to hold the tail down in your bowl while you remove the stuffing with a spoon. If you're eating it at home among friends, don't be afraid to pick up the shell, scoop out the stuffing with your pinky, and then pop it into your mouth.

GUMBOS, BISQUES & SOUPS

Crab and Sweet Potato Bisque

SERVES 5

I think Louisiana chef John Folse created the crab and sweet potato bisque. He's famous throughout America for his elegant takes on traditional Cajun and Creole food. This is my version. It's actually more of a corn and crab bisque with cubed, rather than mashed, sweet potatoes.

- 2 ears corn on the cob
- 450g (1lb) crab shells
- 110g (1/2 cup) butter
- 375g (13oz) lump crab meat
- 1 large sweet potato, peeled and cut into 1cm dice
- 1 small onion, very finely chopped
- 1/4 green pepper, diced
- 1/4 red pepper, diced
- 2 garlic cloves, finely chopped
- 55g (1/3 cup) flour
- 1 bay leaf
- 250ml (1 cup) crème fraîche
- 3 spring onions, finely sliced
- 1 handful of parsley, finely chopped
- zest of 1/2 lemon (optional)
- salt
- black pepper
- cayenne

Cut the whole kernels from the corn cobs into a bowl with a sharp knife. Put half of the corn kernels in a food processor and process to a mush. Simmer the stripped cobs in a pan with a litre (4 cups) of water for 30 minutes, then add the crab shells and simmer for another hour. Strain and keep the stock.

Melt the butter in a very large stockpot over medium-high heat. Add the whole and processed corn kernels, sweet potatoes, onions, red and green pepper and garlic and sauté for 10 minutes. Sprinkle over the flour, then stir until very well combined. Pour in the corn and crab stock, about 120ml (½ cup) at a time, stirring constantly to avoid lumps. Bring the pot to a simmer, then reduce the heat to medium-low and cook for 20 minutes. Add the crème fraîche, spring onions and parsley and simmer for another 5 minutes, then gently stir in the crab meat. Season to taste with salt, pepper and cayenne. Serve the bisque in soup plates, garnished with some lemon zest and parsley.

GUMBOS, BISQUES & SOUPS

Turtle Soup

SERVES 5

My sister Gabrielle is a very picky eater, but her favourite dishes are well-deserving. This is one of them.

I know a lot of people are wary about eating turtle, not being very sure of which ones are endangered and which aren't, but in Louisiana they are a common food. We have three main kinds: snapping turtles, soft shell turtles, and huge alligator snapping turtles.

Snapping turtles are everywhere in Louisiana because we have so much still water around. They love murky, overgrown ponds and ditches and love to come out onto the highway in the summer to sun themselves. I've seen our road home covered with so many turtles that you really have no choice but to run over a few, no matter how horrible you feel about it.

Soft shell turtles are weird creatures. My brother Joel had a collection of live turtles when we were kids and he had a soft shell out in the back yard. The thing bit him one day and left the weirdest, ring-shaped bite I've ever seen. People say these are the best kind to eat, but I can't say I've really eaten enough turtle to tell the difference.

Alligator snapping turtles are monsters. I doubt the stories about them eating pond ducks whole are true, but I do know that if they bite down on your steel-toe boot they'll break your toes. They get up to 75–100lb and can snap your hand off. These, however, are endangered. So if you go to New Orleans and you want to try real Creole-style turtle soup, you'll be served snapping turtle or soft shell turtle.

If you're still not too sure, or can't get hold of any turtle meat, you can easily make a mock turtle soup using the same weight of a mix of beef and veal (and I'll admit here I'm picky about eating veal if I don't know how it's raised – probably my only foodie political stance) or any other meat. You're still gonna get a dang good soup!

This soup can be kept in the refrigerator for up to three days, but reheat only the amounts you are going to use at any one time, as it sours if reheated twice. If the soup gets too thick when it's reheated, add a little cold water.

- 85G (6 TBSP) BUTTER
- 2 TBSP FLOUR
- 225G (8OZ) LEAN HAM, CUT INTO 1 CM CUBES
- 1 LARGE ONION, CHOPPED
- 1 LARGE TOMATO, COARSELY CHOPPED
- 1 TBSP CELERY LEAVES, CHOPPED
- 1 TBSP PARSLEY, FINELY CHOPPED
- 2 GARLIC CLOVES, FINELY CHOPPED
- 2 WHOLE BAY LEAVES, BROKEN IN HALF
- 1/2 TSP DRIED THYME
- 1/2 TSP ALLSPICE
- 450G (1LB) TURTLE MEAT, CUT INTO 1CM CUBES AND KEPT REFRIGERATED
- 350ML (1 1/2 CUPS) RICH BEEF STOCK
- 1 1/2 TSP WORCESTERSHIRE SAUCE
- 1 1/2 TSP WHITE WINE OR SHERRY
- 1 1/2 TSP LEMON JUICE
- SALT
- BLACK PEPPER
- CAYENNE

Begin by making a roux with the butter and flour in a large, heavy pot over medium heat: melt the butter, stir in the flour and keep stirring until it reaches a light brown colour similar to milky coffee or peanut butter (it should take about 10 minutes). Then add the ham, onion, tomato, celery tops, parsley and garlic and stir it all thoroughly. Continue cooking over very low heat until the vegetables soften and brown – about 30 minutes more.

Season well with salt, black pepper and cayenne, then add the bay leaves, thyme and allspice. Put in the turtle meat, then gradually pour in the beef stock and 200ml (a generous 2/3 cup) of water, stirring all the while to keep the soup smooth. Bring it to a boil, then reduce the heat and let the soup simmer for 2 hours, stirring occasionally and scraping the sides and bottom of the pot to prevent scorching. Add the Worcestershire sauce, wine (or sherry, if that's what you're using) and lemon juice. Simmer for 1 hour more.

Let it stand 10 minutes, then stir well before serving.

GUMBOS, BISQUES & SOUPS

Navy Bean Soup

SERVES 4

This has been one of my favourites since I was a kid. Mom makes it fairly often and we normally eat it just as a soup, although many people also like it over rice. As kids we put ketchup in it. Well...

Ingredients:

- 450G (2 1/4 CUPS) DRY WHITE NAVY BEANS, SOAKED OVERNIGHT IN ENOUGH COLD WATER TO COVER
- 225G (8OZ) SMOKED SAUSAGE, FINELY CHOPPED
- 1 LARGE, SLIGHTLY MEATY HAM BONE SAWED INTO 5 CM LENGTHS (YOUR BUTCHER WILL DO THIS IF YOU ASK)
- 1 LARGE ONION, CHOPPED
- 1/2 GREEN PEPPER, CHOPPED
- 2 STALKS CELERY, CHOPPED
- 3 GARLIC CLOVES, FINELY CHOPPED
- 4 SPRING ONIONS, GREEN PARTS ONLY, THINLY SLICED
- 1 TBSP PARSLEY, FINELY MINCED
- 1/4 TSP DRIED THYME
- 1 BAY LEAF, BROKEN IN HALF
- SALT
- BLACK PEPPER
- CAYENNE (I LIKE TO USE BOTH GROUND AND FLAKED CAYENNE IN THIS SOUP)

Drain the beans after soaking them overnight and put them in a large, heavy pot with all the other ingredients. Cover with 2 litres (8 cups) of cold water and bring to the boil, then reduce the heat and simmer for 3 hours. The beans should be very soft and the soup thick. Remove the ham bones from the soup with a slotted spoon.

Remove about 3 cups of whole beans (don't worry if you pick up a few bits of sausage etc as well) and mash them roughly in a bowl with a potato masher before returning to the pot.

Stir the soup well before serving (with ketchup or not).

GUMBOS, BISQUES & SOUPS

Waiting for the gumbo

Meat & Poultry Dishes

Old Boot Sauce	P.72
Rabbit Sauce Piquante	P.73
Smoked Rabbit Sauce Piquante	P.74
Chicken and Sausage Sauce Piquante	P.75
Jambalaya	P.76
Red Beans and Rice	P.77
Mom's New Orleans-Style Daube	P.78
Meatball Stew	P.79
Meat Pie	P.80
Stuffed Duck Breast	P.81
Barbecue with Pops' Barbecue Sauce	P.84
Creole Chicken Fricassee	P.86
Fried Chicken	P.87

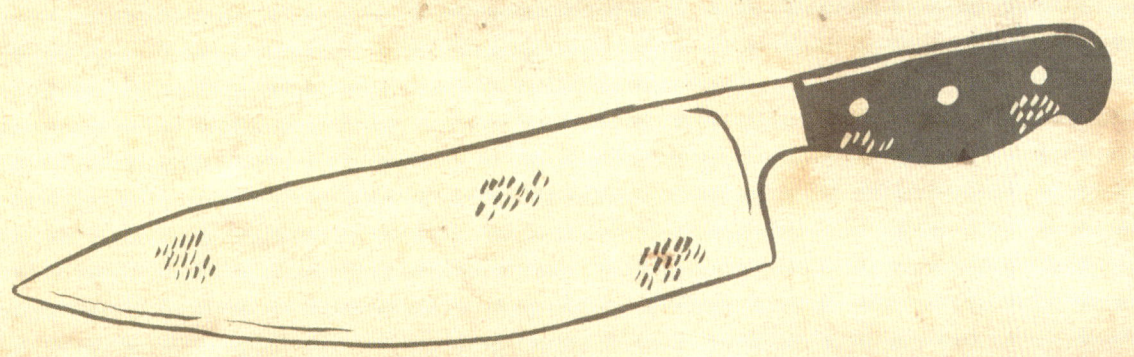

Old Boot Sauce:
A word about pot roasts and gravy

Any time any Cajuns make plans to get together, it starts with, "Hey, let's cook a sauce and play some tunes this weekend!" What kind of sauce is rarely specified unless someone got lucky hunting, took care of a squirrel problem in the yard, or maybe got a gift of some smoked meat. Whatever the meat is, it'll be cooked in a gravy and served over rice. I've seen "sauces" made from chicken wings and necks, but I can't say I've ever gone that far. I call this "Old Boot Sauce" because my dad once joked that he'd eat an old boot if cooked this way.

Pot roast is just a wonderful, simple, delicious thing, and so much can be prepared in the same manner. Normally I use a pork roast, but beef is good, and I also love to prepare chicken thighs this way. To do it, mince a lot of garlic, like maybe 5 or 6 cloves for a nice pork roast, then season the garlic very well with salt and cayenne. Use a sharp knife to cut holes in the meat. With a beef or pork roast, I like to slice a thin tunnel right through the length of it, but with chicken you want to try to get in at the joints or at least close to the bone. I then use my fingers to stuff as much seasoned garlic into the meat as possible. Next you put a bit of vegetable oil in a large, heavy pot, and brown the meat over medium-high heat. Once the meat is nicely browned, add some water to deglaze the pot, and repeat a few times until you get a rich brown liquid from the drippings. Add some little sweet onions, small carrots and new potatoes to the pot if you'd like (but just the meat alone is also perfect if you don't have any vegetables on hand), cover the meat about halfway with water and season with salt, black pepper and cayenne. Cover the pot, turn the heat down to medium-low, and let it simmer. Once the meat is cooked through and very, very tender (you want to let it simmer this way at least an hour, but up to 2 depending on what you're cooking), remove about a coffee cup of the liquid in the pot, stir 1–2 tablespoons of cornstarch into it, pour that back into the pot, and stir a bit. The sauce should thicken up nicely. Serve the pot roast slice over rice.

Gravy in general is so enormously popular that most Cajun kids grow up eating rice and gravy at least twice a day. It's often the first solid food given to a baby. I know my daughter Anna's first solid food was a garlic and cayenne stuffed chicken leg with rice and gravy, and she went to town on it! Zydeco accordionist Cory Ledet was shocked when he played in Russia and, when I translated the menu choices to him, he got "nothing" in reply to his question, "What kinda gravy I get on my rice?" When I want some comfort food, I want mashed potatoes and gravy. I often have a few links of smoked sausage in the freezer and my family loves sausage gravy on rice for dinner. Making a gravy is pretty much the same thing as making a pot roast. You season and brown the meat, let it stick a bit, deglaze the pan with water, and keep going that way until you get the colour you want for the gravy. You can toss in onions and garlic, maybe some green sweet peppers too, and let those cook down with the meat. Then you remove some of the liquid, stir in some cornstarch, pour that back in the pot and stir around to thicken up the sauce. Serve over rice or mashed potatoes (then take the bowl to your room and eat your mashed potatoes and gravy with a spoon like a baby in those weird moments when you're feeling sorry for yourself for no good reason). Pork chops are great for gravy too, and chicken with skin and bone, steaks, or...chicken necks! A lot of people use flour for their gravies, but I find cornstarch mixes better into the liquid and doesn't change the flavour much. If I use flour, I dredge the meat in the flour before browning it, which also thickens the sauce, and gives the gravy a flavour more like roux.

MEAT & POULTRY

Rabbit Sauce Piquante

SERVES 4

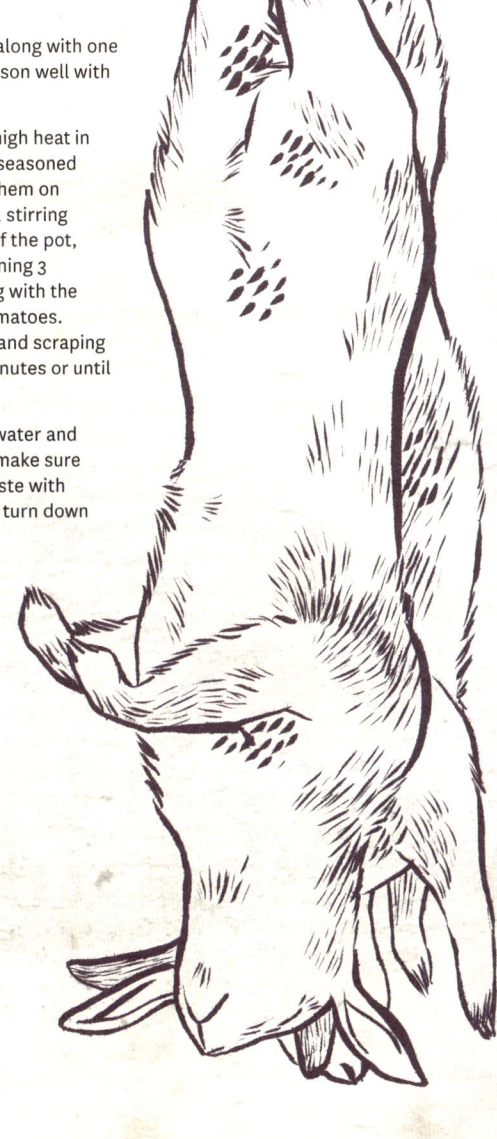

- 1 LARGE RABBIT, JOINTED INTO 6 PIECES
- 2 TBSP OLIVE OIL
- 4 GARLIC CLOVES
- 1 TBSP VEGETABLE OIL
- 110G (3/4 CUP) FLOUR
- 110G (4OZ) SMOKED PORK SAUSAGE, CHOPPED
- 1 MEDIUM ONION, CHOPPED
- 1/2 GREEN PEPPER, CHOPPED
- 4 LARGE TOMATOES, PEELED AND CHOPPED
- 3 SPRING ONIONS, GREEN PARTS ONLY, THINLY SLICED
- HANDFUL OF PARSLEY, FINELY CHOPPED
- SALT
- BLACK PEPPER
- CAYENNE

Toss the rabbit pieces in the olive oil along with one finely chopped clove of garlic and season well with salt, black pepper and cayenne.

Heat the vegetable oil over medium-high heat in a large, heavy pot with a lid. Roll the seasoned rabbit pieces in the flour and brown them on each side. Add the sausage and cook, stirring frequently and scraping the bottom of the pot, for 10 minutes. Finely chop the remaining 3 garlic cloves and add to the pan along with the chopped onion, green pepper and tomatoes. Continue to cook, stirring frequently and scraping the bottom of the pot, for 10 more minutes or until the vegetables are soft.

Add 100ml (a scant half cup) of cold water and scrape the bottom of the pot well to make sure it is deglazed. Season the sauce to taste with salt, black pepper and cayenne, then turn down the heat and leave it to simmer, covered, for 30 minutes. Stir in the spring onions and parsley and cook for 15 minutes more.

Serve over steamed, long grain white rice.

MEAT & POULTRY

Smoked Rabbit Sauce Piquante

SERVES 4

Smoked, roasted rabbit, all cooked and ready to eat, is pretty easy to find at the Chinese stalls at most French markets. It's less easy to find in the UK, but if you can't buy rabbits ready smoked or you want to go all out and smoke your own, it's easy to do at home.

If you don't have $200 to drop on a cold smoker, you can make one for about $10 (but if you do buy a Smoke Daddy, can I come over?). You could build a cold smoker in your yard, using an armoire with any air leaks stuffed with old towels and blankets, shower curtain rods across the top, and an underground tunnel to an outside sunken fire with a trash can lid cover... Oh those crafty Cajuns! Living in Paris, though, I don't have a yard. I am, however, fortunate enough to have a small balcony off of our glassed-in terrace, and on my balcony I have a much-used kettle-style barbecue. I also have a friend from Arkansas who gave me a great tip on rigging up cold smoking at home...

You need a cheap, 40 watt soldering iron, a tin can, and wood chips. Oh, and a sweet little kettle barbecue. Drill or hammer a big hole in the bottom of the tin can, and then some small holes along one side. Fill the can up with hot charcoal to burn out any weird, plastic-y lining, and empty it again. Once it's cool, clean out your barbecue, push your soldering iron into the hole in the bottom of the can, stuff some wood chips around it (I use a mix of pecan wood and apple wood for rabbit, hickory for bacon – both are sold in bags by the same brand as my barbecue), and... take a nap. You'll be at this for a long time.

Ok, well-rested and ready to smoke? Make sure it's chilly outside. You want sweater weather (around 15°C/60°F) so your meat won't spoil while smoking.

For this recipe we're only gonna talk about rabbit. Use a whole rabbit or at least 4 legs. Dry the meat with paper towels, chop up 3–4 cloves of garlic and rub them all over the meat, then season well with salt, black pepper, and cayenne pepper. Give that bunny a deep tissue massage. Let him sit out on the counter like that for about 20 minutes.

Put your can on the bottom of your barbecue, full of wood chips and with foil covering the opening. Lay the rabbit above it, on the top grill of your barbecue. Plug in the soldering iron and close the lid of the barbecue. We're off! (Random side note – I like to put a head or two of garlic on there too. Who doesn't have a hundred uses for smoked garlic?)

So now you stand by and wait about 10 minutes. When you see smoke wisping out of the lid of the grill, unplug the soldering iron. Do not open the lid of the grill. After 30 minutes or so, if you don't see any more smoke, plug the iron back in for another few minutes. You want the wood to smoke, not flame. After about 1½ hours you'll need to refill your can with wood chips – but remember to wear thick gloves when handling the can as it, obviously, will get very hot! Keep going like this for about 6 hours until the rabbit is smoked (it will turn a pretty deep red colour). Make sure the grill stays cold to the touch throughout the smoking process, even at the bottom where the can is resting.

Once your rabbit is nice and smoky, heat 2 tbsp of oil in a large, heavy pot. If you used a whole rabbit, you may want to cut it in half to fit it in the pot. Brown the rabbit on all sides and season it with salt, black pepper and cayenne. Deglaze the pot with a bit of water and repeat the browning-deglazing routine 4 or 5 times until you get a nice, dark gravy. Stir in a teaspoon of cornstarch until it's blended, then add water to cover the rabbit about half way. Cover the pot and simmer very gently for an hour, then turn the rabbit over and simmer for another 30 minutes. Add chopped flat leaf parsley and simmer for another 15 minutes.

Serve over steamed white rice with some sliced tomatoes on the side.

MEAT & POULTRY

Chicken and Sausage Sauce Piquante — SERVES 10

- 1 WHOLE CHICKEN, JOINTED INTO 10 PIECES
- 4 GARLIC CLOVES, 2 CRUSHED WITH THE BACK OF A KNIFE, 2 FINELY CHOPPED
- 30G (2 TBSP) BUTTER
- 1 TBSP PEANUT OR VEGETABLE OIL
- 450G (1LB) SMOKED PORK SAUSAGE
- 4 TBSP PLAIN FLOUR
- 2 ONIONS, FINELY CHOPPED
- 1 GREEN PEPPER, CHOPPED
- 3 LARGE TOMATOES
- 1 TBSP TOMATO PUREE
- SMALL BUNCH OF PARSLEY, CHOPPED
- 6 SPRING ONIONS, GREEN PARTS ONLY, FINELY SLICED
- SALT
- BLACK PEPPER
- CAYENNE

Rub the chicken pieces with the 2 crushed garlic cloves. Season well with salt, black pepper and cayenne.

Heat the butter and oil in a large, heavy saucepan with a lid. Brown the chicken well, letting it stick to the bottom of the pot while browning, then remove it to a plate.

Slice the pork sausage and brown it in the same pot. While it's cooking, dust the chicken pieces lightly with flour and return them to the pot to brown a bit more. After 5 minutes or so, stir in the onions, green pepper and the 2 chopped garlic cloves and cook for 10 minutes, stirring regularly to stop anything burning. Add the peeled and chopped tomatoes to the pot and let them cook down for 15 minutes. Then stir in the tomato purée and 250ml (1 cup) of water and season well with salt, black pepper and cayenne. Cover the pot and simmer for 20 minutes, then throw in the parsley and spring onions, replace the lid and simmer for another 15 minutes.

Serve over steamed, long grain white rice.

MEAT & POULTRY

Jambalaya

SERVES 10

When teaching a French restaurant to make jambalaya, one of the cooks stated the obvious, which had been escaping me for a while: "It's like paella! Easy!" Actually, that probably explains where this dish came from – Louisiana's Spanish settlers – as well as why Louisiana's most popular Jambalaya Cooking Championship takes place in a little town called Gonzales.

The only trick to making jambalaya – and I can not stress this enough – is to really take the time to let the meat stick to the bottom of the pan and then deglaze the pot repeatedly. You can cook the meat for an hour this way if you really want the best texture, most flavour, and richest colour for your jambalaya. You do, don't you?

- 2 TBSP PEANUT OR VEGETABLE OIL
- 900G (2LB) SPICY SMOKED PORK SAUSAGE, SLICED (OR A COMBINATION OF SAUSAGE AND TASSO OR SMOKED, VERY LEAN BACON)
- 1 WHOLE CHICKEN, JOINTED INTO 10 PIECES
- 2 ONIONS, CHOPPED
- 1 GREEN PEPPER, CHOPPED
- 2 CLOVES GARLIC, FINELY CHOPPED
- 400G (2 CUPS) LONG GRAIN WHITE RICE
- 6 SPRING ONIONS, GREEN PARTS ONLY, FINELY SLICED
- SALT
- BLACK PEPPER
- CAYENNE

Heat the oil in a very large, heavy pot with a lid over a medium high heat. When it's hot, put in the sausage. Brown the sausage and cook for 40 minutes or so, regularly pouring in a small amount of cold water and scraping the bottom of the pot well. Put in the chicken pieces and let them brown well all over, then deglaze again with some cold water. When the drippings have reached a deep brown colour, pour off as much fat as you can.

Add the onions, green pepper and garlic and cook until the vegetables are soft, stirring regularly. Season with salt, black pepper and cayenne. Add the rice, stir well, then pour in enough water to cover the rice by 2cm. Bring to a boil, stirring occasionally, and then boil hard until the water cooks off enough to expose the top of the rice. At this point, reduce the heat to low, cover the pot and cook until the rice is tender (about 17 minutes).

Top each serving with sliced spring onions.

Note: A lot of people, including my Uncle Coonie, make this with chicken stock instead of water. The reduced-fat, reduced-salt kind works just as well as the regular. It's very good that way, too, but this recipe is how we do it at home.

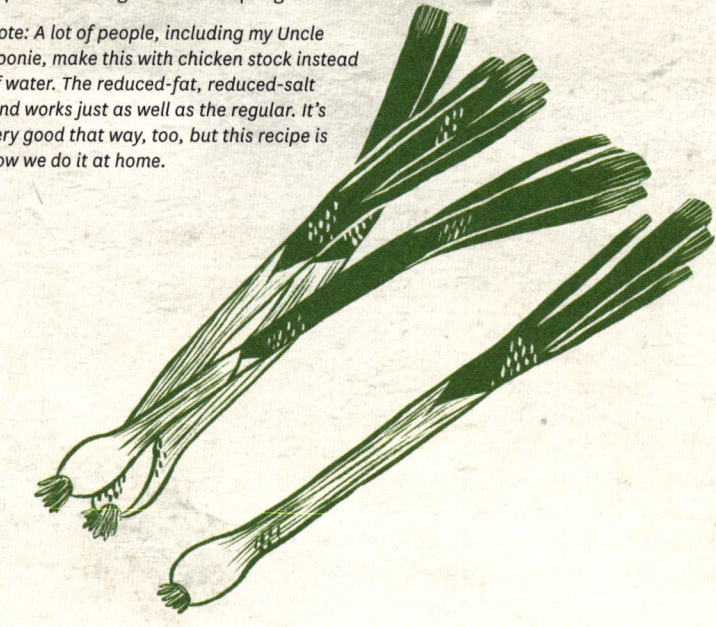

MEAT & POULTRY

Red Beans and Rice

SERVES 6

"Red beans and ricely yours" was how Louis Armstrong signed all his letters, he loved this dish so much. It is the classic New Orleans dish, and perhaps the most famous of all Creole home-style cuisine.

"Pickle meat" is the most important ingredient in red beans and rice. Many people use only smoked ham, tasso, or smoked sausage, but true Creoles will always use "pickle meat". Be sure to rinse it well before adding it to the dish. (Oh, and open a window. Your whole house will smell like vinegar for at least half an hour.)

250ML (1 CUP) DISTILLED WHITE VINEGAR

4 TBSP MUSTARD SEED

1/2 TBSP CELERY SEED

1 TBSP HOT SAUCE

1 BAY LEAF

3 GARLIC CLOVES, PEELED AND SLIGHTLY CRACKED UNDER LIGHT PRESSURE

1/2 TBSP SALT

7 BLACK PEPPERCORNS

250G (9OZ) BONELESS PORK SHOULDER, CUT INTO 2 CM CUBES

Creole-Style Pickle Meat

Put all ingredients but the pork in a saucepan and boil gently for 5 minutes. Leave to cool completely, then add the pork, stirring to remove any air bubbles. Refrigerate for 3 days in a tightly-covered plastic container.

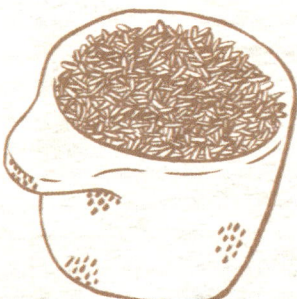

Pickled Onions

Some people like to add pickled onions to their red beans and rice, mixing them into their plates or serving them on the side. To make these, thinly slice 4 large red onions. Put them in a pan with 125ml (½ cup) vinegar, 375ml (1½ cups) water, 1 teaspoon of salt, 2 teaspoons of cayenne, 2 bay leaves, 10 black peppercorns and ½ a teaspoon of dried thyme and boil gently for 5 minutes. Drain the onions and let them sit overnight. The next day, put them in a jar, adding a bit of crushed cayenne. Pour a mixture of 1 part vinegar and 3 parts water over the onions, and keep in the refrigerator at least one week before serving.

250G (1 1/2 CUPS) DRY RED KIDNEY BEANS

3 TBSP VEGETABLE OIL

1 ONION, CHOPPED

1/2 GREEN PEPPER, CHOPPED

3 CELERY STALKS, SLICED

3 CLOVES GARLIC, FINELY CHOPPED

1 QUANTITY PICKLE MEAT (OR 250G (9OZ) SMOKED HAM OR A LARGE SMOKED HAM HOCK)

375G (13OZ) SPICY SMOKED PORK SAUSAGE, SLICED

1 BAY LEAF

5 DASHES HOT SAUCE (OR MORE, TO TASTE)

SALT

BLACK PEPPER

CAYENNE

Red Beans & Rice

Soak the beans in plenty of cold water overnight. The next day, drain and put them in a very large pot, covered with fresh water. Bring to a boil over medium-high heat, checking occasionally to ensure that they remain covered with water). Boil the beans for approximately an hour until they're tender, but don't let them get so soft they fall apart. Drain and return to the pot.

Meanwhile, heat the oil in a frying pan and sauté the onions, green pepper and celery until they're soft. Add the garlic and cook for another 2 minutes, then stir the mixture into the drained beans. Drain the pickle meat (if you're using it) and rinse it really well in cool water, squeezing each piece of meat gently under a running tap. Add it to the beans, along with the sausage and a good seasoning of salt, black pepper and cayenne. Then add the bay leaf and at least 5 dashes of hot sauce and pour in enough cold water to cover.

Bring the pot to a boil over medium-high heat, then reduce heat and simmer for 3 hours, stirring occasionally. "Taste and adjust" for salt, black pepper and cayenne as it cooks.

The beans should thicken considerably in this time. If they don't, remove about a third of them and either mash in a bowl with a potato masher or pulse them briefly in a food processor. Stir the mashed beans back into the pot.

Serve over steamed, long grain white rice.

MEAT & POULTRY

Mom's New Orleans-Style Daube

SERVES 8

If Mom wants to cook something really nice for friends, she cooks daube. This is so delicious I don't have words for it and I'm afraid I don't know how to do it without a slow cooker. It may strike you as odd that the only two slow cooker recipes in this book are Mom's, but please take a moment to consider that she has not only a large house to run, Marc Savoy to feed, numerous projects (such as sewing, photography, drawing and writing books) and no fewer than five bands, but she also has a life of interviews, travelling, friends and four children. Unlike me, slaving away all day in front of a stove is not one of the many ways in which she expresses her creativity.

1–1.5KG (2 1/4 – 3 1/4 LB) TOPSIDE OF BEEF (OR ANY OTHER ROASTING JOINT)

2 TBSP CREOLE SEASONING, SHOP-BOUGHT OR HOMEMADE (SEE PAGE 12)

240ML (1 CUP) ITALIAN SALAD DRESSING

JUICE OF 2 LEMONS

2 TSP HOT SAUCE

2 TBSP VEGETABLE OIL

3 CELERY STALKS, SLICED

1 CARROT, CUT INTO 5CM PIECES

1 ONION, FINELY CHOPPED

3 GARLIC CLOVES, FINELY CHOPPED

4 TBSP ROUX (SEE PAGE 58)

400ML TOMATO PASSATA

1 SMALL BUNCH OF FRESH PARSLEY, FINELY CHOPPED

2 TBSP SUGAR

600G (1LB 5OZ) ANGEL HAIR PASTA

SALT

Day 1

Season the roast by massaging it with Creole seasoning, then marinate it overnight in the Italian salad dressing, lemon juice and hot sauce.

Day 2

Heat 2 tablespoons oil in a large, heavy pot or Dutch oven over a medium-high heat. Remove the meat from the marinade and brown it all over, then transfer it to the slow-cooker. Add the celery, carrot, onion, garlic and the roux, pour over the passata, 750ml (3 cups) water and the reserved marinade and cook the daube on high for 3-4 hours.

Remove the meat from the slow-cooker and leave it, covered with tin foil, to rest for 30 minutes or so.

Add the parsley and sugar to the sauce in the slow-cooker, with more hot sauce and salt to taste. Cook on low while the meat rests.

Boil the pasta according to the package directions and drain.

Using an extremely sharp knife (an electric knife is good if you have one), cut the roast into very thin slices. Transfer any meat debris into the pot with the sauce.

To serve, put the pasta in a large serving dish. Arrange the slices of meat on top and pour over the sauce. Garnish with a little chopped parsley.

MEAT & POULTRY

Meatball Stew

SERVES 6

Some people turn their noses up at this dish, probably in much the same way I did when I first heard of a Meatball Gumbo, but I like it very much and have done since I was a child. What kid doesn't like meatballs? And just because it's cheap to make doesn't mean it's not a good dinner. Thicker than a gumbo but similar in taste, this stew has been a big hit with many of my friends throughout the world.

FOR THE MEATBALLS
450G (1LB) VERY LEAN MINCED BEEF
1 MEDIUM ONION, MINCED
1/2 GREEN PEPPER, MINCED
30G (1/2 CUP) FRESH BREADCRUMBS
1 1/2 TBSP MILK
1 EGG
3 TBSP PARSLEY, FINELY CHOPPED
15 GARLIC CLOVES, EACH ONE CUT IN HALF
1 TBSP VEGETABLE OIL
SALT
BLACK PEPPER
CAYENNE

FOR THE STEW
8 TBSP ROUX
1 LARGE ONION, CHOPPED
1 GREEN PEPPER, CHOPPED
2 CARROTS, CUT INTO THICK SLICES
1 BUNCH OF PARSLEY, FINELY CHOPPED
1 BUNCH OF SPRING ONIONS, FINELY SLICED
SALT
BLACK PEPPER
CAYENNE

Use your hands to mix together the beef, onion, green pepper, breadcrumbs, milk, egg and parsley in a large bowl. Season well with salt, black pepper and cayenne. Form the meat mixture into 30 balls the size of a ping pong ball, and push half a clove of garlic into the centre of each. Heat the oil in a large, heavy frying pan over medium-high heat. Brown the meatballs all over and drain on paper towels.

Now for the stew. Bring 2 litres (8 cups) of water to a gentle boil in a large, heavy stockpot. Reduce the heat to medium, add the roux and stir until it has dissolved, then season to taste with salt, black pepper and cayenne. Stir in the onion, green pepper and carrots and simmer for 20 minutes. If the stew gets above a slow simmer, reduce the heat to medium-low: anything faster will "break" the roux and the sauce will not be thick enough.

Gently drop the meatballs into the stew and simmer for 15 minutes, then add the parsley and spring onions and cook for 15 minutes more.

Serve over steamed, long grain white rice.

MEAT & POULTRY

Meat Pie

MAKES ABOUT 10

Natchitoches, Louisiana, not only has the most brilliant display of Christmas lights throughout the city for its annual Christmas Festival, but is also the home of the Meat Pie Festival, which takes place every September. Natchitoches has been famous for its meat pies since the 1700s and, while there may no longer be street vendors hawking them on each street corner, they can be bought in just about every grocery, café and restaurant in the "Meat Pie Capital".

My friend Dirk Hebert taught me to make my first meat pie. He also taught me a delicious time-saving trick: use canned croissant dough instead of making the pastry. If you want to do this, just pop open the can, knead the dough into a ball, roll it out and cut it into rounds as per the recipe. Rather than frying them, bake the meat pies at 180°C (350°F) for 8-10 minutes. For this recipe you'd need at least 2 cans of croissant dough.

FOR THE FILLING

- 1 tsp butter
- 225g (8oz) lean minced beef
- 225g (8oz) lean minced pork
- 70g (3/4 cup) mushrooms, thinly sliced
- 1 garlic clove, finely chopped
- 1/2 onion, finely chopped
- 1/2 green pepper, finely chopped
- 75g (2 1/2 oz) cream cheese
- Salt
- Black pepper
- Cayenne

FOR THE PASTRY

- 225g (1 1/2 cups) flour
- 1 tsp salt
- 1/2 tsp baking powder
- 45g (3 tbsp) vegetable shortening like Trex
- 1 egg
- 110ml (scant 1/2 cup) milk
- Vegetable oil for deep frying

In a large, deep, heavy skillet, melt the butter over a medium-high heat. Add beef and pork and brown the meat well all over. Stir in the mushrooms, garlic, onion and green pepper, and cook for another 5 minutes. Season very well with salt, black pepper and cayenne, and cook another 8–10 minutes or until the mushrooms are soft. Take the pan off the heat and drain any excess liquid, then stir in the cream cheese. Mix well, and taste for seasonings – it may need some more salt and cayenne.

Leave the filling to cool while you make the pastry. Sift together flour, salt, and baking powder in a large mixing bowl. Use a pastry cutter or two knives to cut in the vegetable shortening until it resembles coarse crumbs.

In a small bowl, beat the egg and milk together and add to the flour mixture, stirring quickly with a knife until you have a dough.

Roll out the pastry dough as thin as you can – about 3mm is perfect – on a floured counter or work surface. Using a 10cm diameter plate as a guide, cut out circles of dough: I get 9 or 10. Place a heaped tablespoon of filling in the middle of one half of the pastry circle and fold the other half over. Brush the edges with water and seal with a fork.

Deep fry the meat pies until they're golden brown, about 7 minutes on each side. Drain on paper towels before serving hot with sliced tomatoes and coleslaw.

MEAT & POULTRY

Stuffed Duck Breast

SERVES 4

Probably nothing beats going out to the fields and bayous at the crack of dawn on a chilly winter morning, bundled up in camouflage, rifles in the back of the truck, brothers and friends chatting happily, sharing bourbon-spiked coffee from a Thermos. Nothing apart from maybe carrying the ducks home with proud smiles and deciding what to do with them – duck gumbo? Baked duck? Duck sauce piquante? Roast duck?

Sometimes you get one that's a bit too… um… hunted-looking to be roasted (I'm talking bullet wounds), so why not remove the breasts to use for this recipe, stew the legs, and use the carcass to make an excellent soup stock for gumbo or whatever else? You can also cook down the fat to make roux if that's to your fancy. Feel your heart slowing down yet?

```
250G (9 OZ) SPINACH
50G (1/3 CUP) PECANS, CHOPPED
(OPTIONAL, AND IF YOU PREFER
ANOTHER NUT TO PECANS, TRY IT!)
50G (1/4 CUP) RAISINS SOAKED IN
BRANDY OVERNIGHT (OR SIMMERED
VERY GENTLY IN DILUTED BRANDY FOR
15 MINUTES)
2 1/2 TBSP DUCK STOCK (IF YOU HAVE
SOME - WATER OR CHICKEN STOCK IS
FINE IF NOT)
1 EGG
30G (1/2 CUP) FRESH BREADCRUMBS
1 TSP PARSLEY, FINELY CHOPPED
4 BONELESS DUCK BREASTS
15G (1 TBSP) BUTTER
SALT
BLACK PEPPER
CAYENNE
```

Wash the spinach well, then cut off any tough stems. Wilt it in a pan with a tight lid over a medium heat, shaking from time to time, for 5 minutes or so. Let the spinach cool, then squeeze out any excess liquid with your hands and chop it roughly. Combine the spinach with the nuts (if you're using them), drained raisins, duck stock, egg, breadcrumbs and parsley and season to taste with salt, black pepper and cayenne.

Use a very sharp, pointed knife to cut a pocket in each duck breast and push a quarter of the spinach stuffing into it. Close the pocket and secure with a toothpick.

In a large frying pan over medium heat, melt the butter and brown the stuffed breasts all over (2–3 minutes on each side). Transfer the breasts to a buttered baking tray and cover them with a greased piece of baking paper. Bake for 7–10 minutes at 200°C (400°F), depending on how much stuffing you squeezed into each breast.

Serve with rice dressing (see page 51) and a salad.

Note: Not that I want to be a bad influence or anything, but you could also consider wrapping the stuffed duck breasts in a thick slice of bacon or rolling them in a mixture of breadcrumbs and finely chopped pecans before cooking.

I would also love to know why Cajuns haven't yet picked up on "fritons" like my husband's family eats in Toulouse. The skin of the duck breast is cut into small pieces and fried in its own fat until crispy. It's the duck version of the pork "gratons" that Cajuns love so much.

MEAT & POULTRY

Just for the fun of it, I'll include here my dad's favourite recipe for roast duck.

He suggests you buy a duck that's lived on the prairie, not one that's been eating frogs and muddy creatures that lend a nasty flavour to the meat.

You stuff the duck with sausage, rice and garlic; lay it on a cedar board (green, so it will smoke in the heat of the oven but won't burn); season it well with salt, black pepper and cayenne; stuff slivers of garlic under the skin; then bake it at 180°C for 40 minutes.

After that, **"you take it out of the oven, toss the duck, and eat the board!"**

Dad tells this joke in one of the many great documentary films by Les Blank's Flower Films. This scene is in the film **"Yum, Yum, Yum!"** (1990), which is all about Louisiana food. It can be ordered online, along with Les's many other excellent, honest, entertaining documentaries about Louisiana life, people, and culture, from **http://www.lesblank.com**. Les passed away only a few months before I finished this book, and his life was celebrated by his friends with lots of great music, garlic and humour.

MEAT & POULTRY

Barbecue with Pops' Barbecue Sauce

Barbecuing in Southwest Louisiana…We sit on the screen porch and leave the yard to the mosquitoes. We swing on one of Dad's hand-crafted cyprus bench swings, talking or reading, with at least two fans blowing some of the 42°C heat away. We drink Mom's iced tea, cold beer, or a gin-and-tonic with lime ("More ice than liquid!" as Mom always orders). Cooking outside keeps the heat out of the kitchen and brings us out of the air conditioning to enjoy life in the big yard around the house—the magnolias and gardenias blooming, the turkeys gobbling, and that quiet that only comes from dead heat in the middle of the summer when most of the Deep South is too lazy to move.

We barbecue home-raised chicken that Dad has slaughtered early that morning, garlic pork sausage, pork ribs, beef steaks, pork chops, salmon and vegetables. All served with with coleslaw, baked beans and Mexican cornbread or another homemade bread.

Pops' Barbecue Sauce

MAKES 500ML (2 CUPS)

This is the barbecue sauce Pops (Grandfather Joel Savoy) used to make. You can't buy barbecue sauce like this at a grocery store: it is good, hearty, chunky and tangy. Often, someone will have a late-night snack of this spread on a thick slice of bread left over from the loaf Mom baked earlier in the day.

Combine all the ingredients in a very heavy, non-reactive pot. Cook the sauce over medium-low heat, stirring occasionally, until it's very thick and the oil has separated out (about 2 hours). Pour off the oil into a bowl and use it to baste meat on the barbecue.

Ingredients

- 125ML (1/2 CUP) VEGETABLE OIL
- 250ML (1 CUP) TOMATO PASSATA
- 1 1/2 LARGE ONIONS, FINELY CHOPPED
- 1/2 LARGE GREEN PEPPER, FINELY CHOPPED
- 2 LARGE CLOVES GARLIC, FINELY CHOPPED
- 1/4 LEMON, THINLY SLICED AND PIPS REMOVED
- 1 HEAPING TBSP BROWN SUGAR
- 2 HEAPING TBSP MUSTARD
- 2 TBSP WORCESTERSHIRE SAUCE
- 1 TSP CAYENNE
- SALT
- BLACK PEPPER

MEAT & POULTRY

Chicken Pieces

Season the chicken pieces all over with a rub of cayenne, freshly ground black pepper, salt, garlic powder and onion powder. You could also marinate them for 3 hours in Italian salad dressing.

Grill the chicken directly over medium heat for about 7 minutes on each side or until the juices run clear. Grill bone-in chicken pieces over direct heat for 3 minutes on each side, then transfer to indirect heat for 10-15 minutes, depending on the size of each piece. The chicken is cooked through when the juices run clear.

Steak and Pork Chops

Rub the meat with a crushed clove of garlic. Season with salt, cayenne, freshly ground black pepper and onion powder. Grill on a direct heat over very hot coals – pork chops should be cooked through but still juicy. How long you grill steaks will depend on the cut, the thickness of the cut and personal preference. I like mine to moo when I cut into it...

Pork Ribs

In a large bowl, whisk together 375ml (1½ cups) pure cane syrup, 60ml (¼ cup) soy sauce, 2 teaspoons country mustard, 60ml (¼ cup) apple cider vinegar, 120ml (½ cup) water, 1 minced onion, 2 minced cloves garlic, ½ teaspoon cayenne, 2½ teaspoons salt, ¼ teaspoon black pepper and 1 small bunch of spring onions, thinly sliced. Put the ribs in a large roasting pan, pour the marinade over them and refrigerate overnight. When you're ready to cook, take the ribs out of the pan, wrap them in foil and grill for an hour, turning them every 15 minutes. Unwrap the ribs, discard the foil, and grill for another 5 minutes on each side.

Vegetables

Marinate mushrooms, cherry tomatoes, chunks of yellow and green pepper, sections of red onion and slices of courgette and aubergine in Italian salad dressing for at least 2 hours. Skewer and grill the vegetables over direct heat for 8-10 minutes or until tender.

Drunk chicken

Rub a whole chicken with olive oil, salt, black pepper and cayenne. Rub the inside with minced garlic and olive oil, then insert a large can of beer (your brand of choice) into the body of the chicken. Stand the chicken (beer can upright) on the barbecue over indirect heat and cook, covered, for 45-60 minutes or until it's cooked through.

Swamp Kebabs

In 2011 I was invited to the Grillstock Festival in Bristol, England. Large, built men in muscle shirts were slinging huge, bloody slabs of meat onto barbecues of various sizes and power throughout the festival grounds – obviously not a crowd we find at most other festivals! I played a fun set with the Francadians on the main stage, then clicked off, beer in hand, to the Newman's Own BBQ Academy cooking tent to grill alligator! The festival-organisers had found alligator tail steaks from an online source and had them delivered, frozen and vacuum-packed. So I used Pops' Barbecue Sauce to make these swamp kebabs:

Debone a large alligator tail steak and cut it into chunks. Slice 450g (1lb) smoked pork sausage into chunks, and roughly chop up some red and yellow peppers and a large onion. Spear the ingredients onto metal skewers, playing with the colours and going for a pattern like alligator, pepper, sausage, onion, repeat.

Brush the kebabs with olive oil and season with salt, black pepper and cayenne, then grill over medium-high heat for 3-5 minutes on each side or until they're done, basting with barbecue sauce as they cook.

MEAT & POULTRY

Creole Chicken Fricassee

SERVES 8

- 4 tbsp flour
- Pinch of garlic powder
- Pinch of onion powder
- Pinch of dried thyme
- The slightest dash of allspice
- 1 chicken, jointed into 10 pieces
- 45g (3 tbsp) butter
- 2 large onions, chopped
- 3 garlic cloves, finely chopped
- 2 stalks celery, strings removed and sliced
- 1 carrot, sliced
- 375ml (1 1/2 cups) beer
- 3 tbsp roux (see p.58)
- 1 tsp Worcestershire sauce
- Small bunch of parsley, finely chopped
- Salt
- Black pepper
- Cayenne

Season the flour with ½ teaspoon of salt, ¼ teaspoon of black pepper, ¼ teaspoon of cayenne and the garlic powder, onion powder, dried thyme and allspice. Spread the seasoned flour on a large plate and dust the chicken pieces all over. In a large, heavy pot with a lid, melt 2 tablespoons of the butter over medium-high heat and brown the chicken pieces nicely all over.

While the chicken is browning, melt the remaining tablespoon of butter in a frying pan and sauté the onion, garlic, celery and carrot for about 8 minutes or until the vegetables start to soften. Remove from the heat.

Once the chicken is nicely browned, put it on a plate and pour the beer and 125ml (½ cup) of water into the pot, scraping up any residue stuck to the bottom.

Stir the roux into the beer and water and continue stirring until it's incorporated. Return the chicken pieces to the pot, along with the softened vegetables and a teaspoon of Worcestershire sauce. Bring to a gentle simmer, stirring occasionally, then cover the pot and cook for 25 minutes. Taste and season with salt, black pepper and cayenne.

To serve, arrange the chicken pieces on plates over steamed, long grain white rice and spoon the gravy generously over each portion. Garnish with chopped parsley.

MEAT & POULTRY

Fried Chicken

There are many things I often just assume people know how to do because I grew up doing them, and I'm often surprised when people say, "Oh my goodness, how did you make this [insert any ordinary dish here, like fried chicken, meatloaf, etc.]?"

So let me just toss in this one random soul food comfort meal. Serve it up with mashed potatoes, a side of corn macque choux (see page 43), and maybe biscuits and gravy! To stop it being a complete carb overload, smothered okra (page 44) is also great with fried chicken.

Note: you can either fry the chicken wings as well, or freeze them to make hot wings another day.

---

1 WHOLE CHICKEN, JOINTED INTO 10 PIECES

500ML (2 CUPS) BUTTERMILK

1 TSP DRY MUSTARD

1/2 TSP THYME

A DASH OF HOT SAUCE (OR MORE TO TASTE)

300G (2 CUPS) PLAIN FLOUR

SALT

BLACK PEPPER

CAYENNE

VEGETABLE OIL FOR FRYING

Put the chicken pieces in a bowl with the buttermilk and add the dry mustard, thyme and a dash of hot sauce. Season the chicken with salt, black pepper and cayenne and mix well, then leave it in the fridge for at least 1½ hours, turning the pieces every 30 minutes.

Pour off as much of the buttermilk as you can, then mix the flour in with the chicken pieces to coat them. The batter will be very sticky and moist.

Preheat the oven to 150°C (300°F). Fill a deep, heavy-bottomed skillet with enough oil to cover the largest piece of chicken and heat the oil until it's hot but not smoking. Working in batches, place the chicken pieces in the oil and fry on each side for at least 8 minutes or until the juices run clear when you pierce near the bone with a small, sharp knife. Thighs take the longest – up to 20 minutes a side. Once cooked, remove the pieces, drain them on a bed of paper towels and transfer to the oven for only as long as it takes you to cook the other pieces.

While you've got the oil hot, why not mix up a batch of hush puppies to eat with the chicken? Mix up 240g (1½ cups) of cornmeal, 110g (¾ cup) of flour, ½ teaspoon of bicarbonate of soda, ½ teaspoon of baking powder, ½ teaspoon of salt, ½ a small onion (finely chopped), 250ml (1 cup) of milk or buttermilk, and an egg. Throw in some chopped jalapeños or crab meat if you have any and drop the batter by tablespoons into the hot oil. Fry on all sides until golden brown and drain on paper towels.

MEAT & POULTRY

Fish & Seafood

Prawn Creole	P.90
Marc Savoy's Seafood Medley Courtbouillon	P.91
Aubergine Pirogue	P.101
Crayfish Etouffee	P.102
Atchafalaya Special Fried Fish with Crayfish Etouffee Topping	P.104
Crayfish Pie	P.105
Crayfish Enchiladas	P.106
Crayfish Fettuccine	P.107
Crab Cakes Savoy	P.108
Oysters Rockefeller	P.110
Oysters Savoy	P.111
Beer Batter and PoBoys	P.112

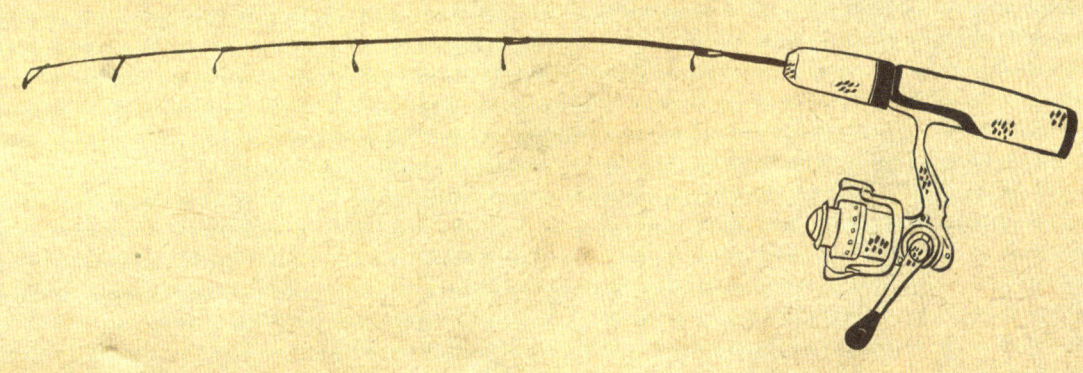

Prawn Creole

SERVES 4

- 3 tbsp plain flour
- 45g (3 tbsp) butter
- 2 medium onions, finely chopped
- 3 stalks celery, finely chopped
- 1 green pepper, chopped
- 2 cloves garlic, finely chopped
- 1 bay leaf
- 750g (1lb 10oz) large uncooked prawns, peeled, heads and tails removed
- 4 tomatoes, peeled and chopped
- 60ml (1/4 cup) white wine
- 4 spring onions, sliced
- salt
- black pepper
- cayenne

In a large frying pan, cook the flour in the oil over medium-high heat to make a medium-brown roux. Keep stirring all the time to prevent it from burning. Carefully stir in the onions, celery, green pepper and garlic (the oil will splatter as you put them in). Season with salt, cayenne, and just a touch of black pepper. Cook, stirring frequently, until the vegetables are wilted.

Pour in 125ml (½ cup) of water and the bay leaf and stir well. Add the prawns, tomatoes and white wine and cook, stirring frequently, for 5–7 minutes until the prawns are pink and cooked through. The sauce should be thick but not dry so add a little more water if you need to. Taste and season with more salt, black pepper and cayenne as necessary.

Serve over steamed, long grain white rice and scatter with sliced spring onions.

FISH & SEAFOOD

Marc Savoy's Seafood Medley Courtbouillon

SERVES 5

This is my youngest brother Wilson's favourite. It's a delicious dish that's quite pleasing to the eye—artful right from the start. Though we often cook it outside over a burner or raised above an open fire, it's great on a stove too (although you'll miss the smoky flavour from the open fire that way). We used to make this using catfish, but Louisiana waterways have become too polluted to provide tasty fish these days, sadly. If you can get Spotted Catfish that is fresh and doesn't smell oily, muddy, or otherwise unpleasant, go ahead and use it. Lately, we buy cod fillets, but any type of firm white-fleshed fish is good. My dad also once made a courtbouillon using perch from the Gulf of Mexico and I preferred it to catfish.

An important rule when making courtbouillon—NEVER stir it. This not only interrupts the cooking process (you shouldn't take the lid off for the first 30 minutes of cooking time except to make sure it's only simmering very gently) but also breaks up the fish. As my dad says, "You want to make sure you never get invited back to a courtbouillon dinner? Just go walk up and stir around in the pot. A lot of old Cajuns would throw you right out of the party for something like that!"

1/2 TBSP VEGETABLE OIL

1 MEDIUM ONION, CHOPPED

1/2 GREEN PEPPER, CHOPPED

1 GARLIC CLOVE, FINELY CHOPPED

750G (1LB 10OZ) COD FILLETS (TRY TO CHOOSE THICKER ONES), CUT INTO 6CM PIECES

250G (9OZ) LARGE PRAWNS, PEELED AND DEVEINED

250G (9OZ) LARGE SCALLOPS

1 1/2 TBSP FLOUR

1/2 TSP SALT

1/2 TSP BLACK PEPPER

1/2 TSP CAYENNE

125ML (1/2 CUP) TOMATO PASSATA

1 SMALL BUNCH OF SPRING ONIONS, SLICED

1 SMALL BUNCH OF PARSLEY, CHOPPED

Heat the vegetable oil over medium heat in a big heavy pot with a lid. Use about a third of the chopped onion, green pepper and garlic to make a layer on the bottom of the pot. Follow this with a loose layer of a mix of about a third of the cod, prawns and scallops. Put the flour, salt, black pepper and cayenne in a small cup and mix together, then sprinkle a third of it over the fish/seafood layer. Drizzle everything with a third of the passata and 4 teaspoons of water, then repeat the layering process twice more.

Cover the pot and let the dish come to a gentle simmer. Simmer over a low heat for about 35 minutes, until the vegetables have mostly sunk to the bottom. Scatter over the spring onions and parsley, put the lid back on and cook for another 5 minutes.

Serve the courtbouillon over steamed, long grain white rice.

As my dad promised when teaching me to make this dish, "That's the recipe for the most fantastic courtbouillon you'll ever eat in your life!"

FISH & SEAFOOD

I'm including here a project I did on assignment from my Louisiana Folklore class when I was 20. I love re-reading this from time to time, as it puts me right back in the kitchen. You'll notice, if you read it, that I've repeated a lot of the same things in this book that are in the essay, but I'm leaving it just the way I turned it in. (And, yes, I got an A.)

Catfish Courtbouillon,
a cooking interview with
Marc Savoy & Albert Rozas

I skipped work Friday afternoon to drive out to Eunice. The original plan was to go out to the woods behind my parents' home to cook a catfish courtbouillon with my dad Marc Savoy, my mom Ann Savoy and their friends Albert Rozas, and Tina Pilione. The rain pushed our plan into my mom's kitchen.

Marc Savoy The first thing is the right kind of fish. We don't want to use fish fillets. You don't want to use pond-raised catfish because that doesn't make a very good courtbouillon. You want to use a fish with the bones in it. We always try to get a spotted cat, which is also called an Opelousas cat, because it's a much better fish. The reason why it's better is because it's not a scavenger like the blue cats or channel cats are. You want to catch them you have to fish them with live bait. They won't eat on dead bait. The result of that is that the flesh is a lot sweeter, a lot less oily. We always try to use that. It's our favourite. It's totally shaped different, too. They do have little spots on them. They're a different colour. They're not shaped like a shark like the blue cat. The spotted cat is flat; it has a flat head.

We always try to take the belly off which is real succulent flesh and there's no bones in that and we'll use that to fry. And the other part is what we're gonna make the courtbouillon from. We cut up a whole bunch of onions, garlic, and bell peppers. The way that I learned how to make a courtbouillon was from my father. What he would do, he'd put a real light film of cooking oil in the bottom of the pot. Sort of like, grease the bottom of the pot. He would put a layer of fish into the bottom of the pot, sprinkle a little bit of white flour, sprinkle some salt, black pepper and red pepper, then the vegetables mixture, and repeat the process. The white flour is for the gravy. Repeat this until there's no more fish or the pot's full. We always tried to cook this outside because it tastes much better cooked over an open fire. We would make a fire with oak because it makes coals. A lot of wood that you burn doesn't make coals, but oak makes very good, very, very hot coals. We make the fire, but we don't put the pot on the fire immediately because you don't want to put it on while it's flaming. You make the coals and when the fire just about goes out and there's just some glowing red coals, then you put your cast iron pot on top of that. Real low heat. You don't want to heat it up too fast.

FISH & SEAFOOD

	I'd usually start with the lid on top of the pot because if you do that – don't add water, only one can of tomato sauce in a #14 cast iron pot – if you start it real slowly with the lid on, it begins to steam inside the pot and the juice comes out of the onions and bell peppers, parsley and onion tops, and it begins to make a gravy. You cook it very, very slowly with all these ingredients inside.
	And you never, never stir inside the pot. A lot of these old black pots have rings or handles. You take the handles and you twist it counter clockwise and clockwise. You take it off the coals and you give it a twist. You never, ever stir it. You want to insult a lot of these old Cajuns, when you want to serve yourself the food, you go stir it in the pot. That's a good way either get thrown out of the party all together or never to be invited again. When it's just about cooked, then you can take the lid off and let it make sort of like a thick cream on top. It doesn't have to cook that long. For a large pot of fish, maybe like only 30-45 minutes after it starts boiling. And that's the recipe for the most fantastic courtbouillon you'll ever eat in your life.
Ann Savoy	Tell her about the rice, too.
Marc	The rice is the same way. You start the rice on a real high heat. All of this is done in real thick cast iron pots. You start it uncovered, on a real high heat. My measurement is fill up the pot with rice and put the water up to the first ring of your finger over the rice and a little bit of salt. That's all you have to do. You cook it real fast. It has to come to a boil real, real fast because if it doesn't your rice is going to be real, real mushy. So what we do we start it on a real high heat and it boils. Then as soon as all the rice is boiled off the top, you put the lid on and lower the heat by getting rid of some of the coals. Get a stick and push out some of the coals. You want to let it cook very slowly.
Albert Rozas	I grew up in Choupique. It means fish. Tonight we knew it was gonna rain, so I went ahead and got a jump on it and made the gravy ahead of time. I put in very little water. I just washed out the tomato sauce can. Ha ha. I put one can of water. Choupique is a scaled fish. It's very plentiful in the bayous and in this area. I don't know where the name originated. The place is about two and a half miles southeast of Chatagnier. I cooked outside a lot. My dad taught me. We do it the exact same way Marc did. Why change it? It's good.
Marc	The people in Lafayette put tomato paste in it. They put tomato paste and tomato paste and tomato paste.
Albert	I know!
Marc	I remember, my father had gone to cook some fish in Washington, Louisiana. He was telling us about a guy from Scott. He watched him open 14 cans of tomato paste. 14 cans. Dad said, "What are you doing?" And the guy said, "I'm making a sauce." The guy said, "Isn't that what you cook?" And Daddy said, "No, we don't cook it that way." So the guy said, "When you cook I want to go watch you." So when Daddy started cooking the guy came over to watch and Daddy opened one can of sauce. The guy said, "Well, that's all you're gonna put?" And Daddy said, "Yeah." So after it was cooked Daddy went to sample it and said it was uneatable and so sour with all the cans of tomatoes. And then he said the guy came and said, "Let me taste yours." And the guy said, "Gah-lee, well that's a lot better than mine!" You know, for a cook to admit that.
Albert	See, I don't know if you can see the colour, but it's not red, it's pink.

FISH & SEAFOOD

	It's not red. And then when we put the fish it's gonna get even more pinkish. You don't want it to be red. And Marc, you need to tell her about the gratin.
Marc	Oh yeah! The gratin!
Sarah	I don't like gratin.
Marc	You don't like gratin?!?! You must not be related to me!
Albert	It is so good with fish. It should be against the law to eat fish without gratin.
	We fish a lot in bayous. I used to go on my bicycle when I was a boy and the water wasn't as polluted as it is today. I'd come back with fish in my basket on my bicycle and I furnished fish for my dad's family and my mom's family for quite a few years. But now we fish a little further south in the Intracoastal Canal. I have a little camp and we catch fish. We probably consume at least 500 pounds of fish per year. We grew our own vegetables in the garden. Garlic, onions, bell peppers – I planted the elephant garlic one year, but I didn't like it. It wasn't as strong as the smaller garlic.
Marc	Albert, where'd you get that pot?
Albert	I won that pot when I was in the Boy Scouts. That was a long time ago. There was a parade in Ville Platte. I lived in Evangeline Parish and there was a parade. We did a cookout on the bed of a big flatbed truck. We had a big tub, a washtub, and we built the fire in the tub. We cooked while the parade was going on. We came out first and I won that pot. I was probably nine or ten years old. I was born in 1943. Marc and I grew up together. He's much older than I am. I can only say that 'cause he stepped out of the room.
Ann	Tell more about the cast iron, Albert.
Albert	This is the old-time cast iron. You feel how heavy that is? It's not the same as they make them today. It's a different cast. This cast is tight. The newer pots are more porous. You can tell it's different. You have to burn them before you use them. I grease mine with hog lard. You put it in the open fire. We call that seasoning the pot. If you do it that way you can wash it and it won't rust. You can re-do it, too, if you have a rusted one. You can use vegetable oil too, but I was taught to use hog lard, so that's what I do.
Marc	This pot here was my momma's momma's pot. The other ones we have are from the Fifties. Sarah, you really need to stress the importance of the fish. Here's a good picture. That's me cleaning the fish.
Sarah	That's not fish guts. That's a pig.
Marc	No, that's the fish.
Sarah	No, it must be a pig. It's too big.
Marc	No, that's the fish.
Sarah	Well, how big a fish is it?
Marc	It's about that long (holding hands about 4½ feet apart). That's the guts.
Albert	Blue cat's pretty good fried, but in a gravy you can't beat the spotted cat. The reason we're cooking blue cat tonight is because spotted cat's hard to find this time of year.

FISH & SEAFOOD

Marc	You can't raise spotted cat in a pond.
Albert	Yeah, they have to be in the bayou. They're wild. They usually weigh 10–15 pounds. The biggest one I caught was 53 pounds. It's best to use the 10–15 pound ones to make a gravy, though. Sometimes you hear about people catching ones that weigh a hundred and something pounds.
Marc	In the Nile they can get over 200 pounds.
Albert	An old man caught one 287 pounds in the Atchafalaya Basin. He caught that in a net. The best time for fishing is in the spring, but we catch spotted cat all summer long until the fall.
Marc	When you take the lid off, the smoke from the wood goes into the pot and gives the food a smoked taste.
Albert	The whole ordeal is just fun. It's so much fun to cook outside. It was normally just the men. Sometimes those things weren't planned. Sometimes we'd just meet up around 3:00 in the afternoon and say, "Hey, let's go cook some fish." So we'd go find some fish and just cook it right there. Spur of the moment, you know? The women sometimes came with us, but the men did the fishing usually. Most women didn't like to do that. Rose always came fishing and hunting with me.
Marc	The spotted cat is real flat and the blue cat is shaped like a torpedo.
Albert	There are some cats that are yellow, yellow, yellow…
Marc	Boy, those were good to eat. You don't see that in the bayou any more.
Albert	No, the last time we caught some was at the Channel 3 Tower. We'd go over there with some chicken hearts in the spring. Man, we'd mop up. We'd catch them and we'd cook them right away. The water used to be clean. You could eat them like that.
Ann	Tell about that, Albert.
Albert	You could eat fish from anywhere. It's not like that any more. There's a lot of places now you can only eat fish so many times a month. Expectant women can't eat fish from a certain area any more. If you're younger than seven or nine years old, the Wildlife & Fisheries committee will tell you, don't eat the fish from a certain body of water. And there's a lot of bodies of water in Louisiana that are that way. They're polluted by farming, chemicals, acid rain… It wasn't like that when I was young. No, no. You could eat fish from anywhere in those days and it was good and it was healthy.
Marc	When your mommy and I played in Breaux Bridge, Sarah, and Mary, from Peter, Paul and Mary, came to meet us and came over to eat. Red Bird had given us a lot of fish to eat. I went in the barn and cleaned one for Mary and her husband and it was so stinky and so oily. It was so bad! Supposedly it was from the Calcasieu, and we were so disappointed. You know, wow, Albert and I used to swear by the fish from the Calcasieu. When I skinned that one fish I could not get that smell off my hands. And when we cooked it the whole house smelled like that. I went and threw the whole box away. I couldn't eat it. I was telling that to Albert. I said, "Man, that fish from the Calcasieu was bad! It was uneatable!" He said, "Really?" So he has a brother that lives in Lake Charles that gets fish from Red Bird. So guess what, that fish that Red Bird had given me, Albert found out from his brother, did not come from the Calcasieu. It came from a bayou that he was fishing in. His brother had had the same experience. So, the Calcasieu above

FISH & SEAFOOD

	Lake Charles is good, at least.
Tina	Lake Charles has oil refineries and chemical companies.
Albert	Now we're gonna layer the fish. We always try and put the thickest pieces of fish at the bottom because it's gonna take longer to cook.
Marc	I want to say something about catching spotted cat. They only bite on live bait, so if you want to catch them you can't, you know... most of the blue cat, you fish with a piece of rotten meat and they'll bite on that. Even soap – they'll bite on anything. But spotted cat, a lot of times, it's been known that a lot of times, people caught a small fish, like a small blue cat on a rotten piece of bait, then a huge spotted cat goes and feeds on the little blue cat.
Sarah	Do you have any stories about this, Albert?
Albert	The only story I have is that it's good.
Marc	My daddy said that he and one of the neighbours over here, a big, big eater... He loved to eat and he could eat – I remember the old man very well, Noah Young. He'd eat like five men and he was also a great cook. They'd bring this old man to cook when they'd go fishing. He'd always bring all his ingredients in a big dishpan. After he had everything cooked, when people started serving themselves, he'd say, "Dad-gummit! I forgot my plate at home!" And he'd always do that. He did it on purpose. He'd say, "Dog-gone! I forgot my plate. I guess I'll have to eat out of the dishpan." He'd forget his plate on purpose so he could eat out of the dishpan. That way nobody could see how much he was eating. And he'd eat and eat and eat.
Albert	Now this is the last time this pot is going to see a spoon. It's boiling at the right speed now, real slow. I used a spoon to get that fish down under the gravy a little more. I'm going to cover it now and let it cook.
Marc	Albert, tell Sarah about when you went hand fishing.
Albert	It was bad at first. I remember I had the jitters at first.
Marc	Yeah, you just drank a lot of beer and you were okay...
Albert	I went with Polan, Marc, you remember Polan?
Marc	Yeah.
Albert	I went with Polan to go hand fishing. I was in the boat and he was doing the hand fishing and all of a sudden he says, "You'll have to come in." There's a bunch of fish. There was a sink, like a hole in the bank. He says, "You'll have to go in the other end. It's too big. I can't get the other side." I got down and I went in the water and I felt the hole. And man! All of a sudden I put my hand in there and there were fish just floating around all over the place! And I looked up and there was this branch over my head and there was a snake about this big (about a two inch diameter) and I think I walked on water. I didn't stop till I got to the boat. Man! That snake scared me! And he caught enough for us to eat, but I told him, "I'm not going back in that water. That's it, that snake scared me.
Marc	Albert, tell Sarah about that time we had gone with the dynamite to catch all that fish. Remember?
Albert	Oh, my God! (laughs) I don't know if we should say that... (laughs more) Yeah.

FISH & SEAFOOD

Marc	You can't raise spotted cat in a pond.
Albert	Yeah, they have to be in the bayou. They're wild. They usually weigh 10-15 pounds. The biggest one I caught was 53 pounds. It's best to use the 10-15 pound ones to make a gravy, though. Sometimes you hear about people catching ones that weigh a hundred and something pounds.
Marc	In the Nile they can get over 200 pounds.
Albert	An old man caught one 287 pounds in the Atchafalaya Basin. He caught that in a net. The best time for fishing is in the spring, but we catch spotted cat all summer long until the fall.
Marc	When you take the lid off, the smoke from the wood goes into the pot and gives the food a smoked taste.
Albert	The whole ordeal is just fun. It's so much fun to cook outside. It was normally just the men. Sometimes those things weren't planned. Sometimes we'd just meet up around 3:00 in the afternoon and say, "Hey, let's go cook some fish." So we'd go find some fish and just cook it right there. Spur of the moment, you know? The women sometimes came with us, but the men did the fishing usually. Most women didn't like to do that. Rose always came fishing and hunting with me.
Marc	The spotted cat is real flat and the blue cat is shaped like a torpedo.
Albert	There are some cats that are yellow, yellow, yellow…
Marc	Boy, those were good to eat. You don't see that in the bayou any more.
Albert	No, the last time we caught some was at the Channel 3 Tower. We'd go over there with some chicken hearts in the spring. Man, we'd mop up. We'd catch them and we'd cook them right away. The water used to be clean. You could eat them like that.
Ann	Tell about that, Albert.
Albert	You could eat fish from anywhere. It's not like that any more. There's a lot of places now you can only eat fish so many times a month. Expectant women can't eat fish from a certain area any more. If you're younger than seven or nine years old, the Wildlife & Fisheries committee will tell you, don't eat the fish from a certain body of water. And there's a lot of bodies of water in Louisiana that are that way. They're polluted by farming, chemicals, acid rain… It wasn't like that when I was young. No, no. You could eat fish from anywhere in those days and it was good and it was healthy.
Marc	When your mommy and I played in Breaux Bridge, Sarah, and Mary, from Peter, Paul and Mary, came to meet us and came over to eat, Red Bird had given us a lot of fish to eat. I went in the barn and cleaned one for Mary and her husband and it was so stinky and so oily. It was so bad! Supposedly it was from the Calcasieu, and we were so disappointed. You know, wow, Albert and I used to swear by the fish from the Calcasieu. When I skinned that one fish I could not get that smell off my hands. And when we cooked it the whole house smelled like that. I went and threw the whole box away. I couldn't eat it. I was telling that to Albert. I said, "Man, that fish from the Calcasieu was bad! It was uneatable!" He said, "Really?" So he has a brother that lives in Lake Charles that gets fish from Red Bird. So guess what, that fish that Red Bird had given me, Albert found out from his brother, did not come from the Calcasieu. It came from a bayou that he was fishing in. His brother had had the same experience. So, the Calcasieu above

FISH & SEAFOOD

	Lake Charles is good, at least.
Tina	Lake Charles has oil refineries and chemical companies.
Albert	Now we're gonna layer the fish. We always try and put the thickest pieces of fish at the bottom because it's gonna take longer to cook.
Marc	I want to say something about catching spotted cat. They only bite on live bait, so if you want to catch them you can't, you know... most of the blue cat, you fish with a piece of rotten meat and they'll bite on that. Even soap – they'll bite on anything. But spotted cat, a lot of times, it's been known that a lot of times, people caught a small fish, like a small blue cat on a rotten piece of bait, then a huge spotted cat goes and feeds on the little blue cat.
Sarah	Do you have any stories about this, Albert?
Albert	The only story I have is that it's good.
Marc	My daddy said that he and one of the neighbours over here, a big, big eater... He loved to eat and he could eat – I remember the old man very well, Noah Young. He'd eat like five men and he was also a great cook. They'd bring this old man to cook when they'd go fishing. He'd always bring all his ingredients in a big dishpan. After he had everything cooked, when people started serving themselves, he'd say, "Dad-gummit! I forgot my plate at home!" And he'd always do that. He did it on purpose. He'd say, "Dog-gone! I forgot my plate. I guess I'll have to eat out of the dishpan." He'd forget his plate on purpose so he could eat out of the dishpan. That way no body could see how much he was eating. And he'd eat and eat and eat.
Albert	Now this is the last time this pot is going to see a spoon. It's boiling at the right speed now, real slow. I used a spoon to get that fish down under the gravy a little more. I'm going to cover it now and let it cook.
Marc	Albert, tell Sarah about when you went hand fishing.
Albert	It was bad at first. I remember I had the jitters at first.
Marc	Yeah, you just drank a lot of beer and you were okay...
Albert	I went with Polan, Marc, you remember Polan?
Marc	Yeah.
Albert	I went with Polan to go hand fishing. I was in the boat and he was doing the hand fishing and all of a sudden he says, "You'll have to come in." There's a bunch of fish. There was a sink, like a hole in the bank. He says, "You'll have to go in the other end. It's too big. I can't get the other side." I got down and I went in the water and I felt the hole. And man! All of a sudden I put my hand in there and there were fish just floating around all over the place! And I looked up and there was this branch over my head and there was a snake about this big (about a two inch diameter) and I think I walked on water. I didn't stop till I got to the boat. Man! That snake scared me! And he caught enough for us to eat, but I told him, "I'm not going back in that water. That's it, that snake scared me.
Marc	Albert, tell Sarah about that time we had gone with the dynamite to catch all that fish. Remember?
Albert	Oh, my God! (laughs) I don't know if we should say that... (laughs more) Yeah.

FISH & SEAFOOD

Marc	They had this deep hole...
Albert	Yeah, before we went with the dynamite – it's a good thing that keg of Carbide didn't go off because... you remember that?
Marc	Oh, yeah, I remember that!
Albert	Yeah, Marc had got a keg of Carbide from his dad. It didn't go off and it's a good thing. I think maybe it was too old or something.
Sarah	Carbide? What is that?
Marc	It's an element. When it hits the water it creates a gas and if you can figure out a way to ignite it it'll blow up.
Albert	It causes a concussion and it breaks the insides of the fish and they float.
Marc	We'd run. We'd throw the Carbide in the water and we'd run, you'd swear like–
Albert	You don't need a lot of Carbide to do this. My dad told me after this incident that they'd use some little cans (gesturing about half a litre). We had about a five gallon drum – a keg. If that thing would have went off they'd still be raking our pieces out from around there.
	(Marc laughing in the background.)
Albert	We weren't supposed to use that much.
Marc	Where was that, Albert?
Albert	Place Fabousse
Marc	I don't remember it.
Albert	It's on the other side of where y'all went to get that tree. It's a little bit west of that.
Marc	Bayou de Cane.
Albert	Bayou de Cane, yep, there was a big deep hole.
Marc	That was a long time ago, huh Albert? When was that?
Albert	It was a long time ago. And it was far. We had to drag the boat through the woods.
Marc	I guess it was about thirty-five years ago.
Albert	I was in back of the boat, Marc was in front. Sometimes I think he would drag the boat and me. *(Everyone laughing)*
Albert	Anyway, that didn't work so we got together with a friend of ours, Dore Frugé, and he got us some dynamite. And we went there one day and, man, let me tell you something – the water flew and I don't remember how high–
Marc	I think we put one stick with a blasting cap and we threw that in there–
Albert	Oh, no, we–
Marc	No, but then we tried two sticks and nothing happened again. So I told that to Albert, I said, "We're gonna tape it all up". So we taped–
Albert	It was a pack of dynamite that big! (gesturing about a ten inch circle)
Marc	We must have had seven or eight sticks and we'd run! We'd hide

FISH & SEAFOOD

	behind the cars. So when we taped the whole thing together – let me tell you – everything came out, some logs… We just blew up the whole thing. And you know what came out? We got one – after all the water cleared out, only one old bullfrog came out to the top, just paddling away, looking around, seeing what was happening, you know, not a fish.
Albert	Normally, though, some people got a lot of fish that way. But I remember somebody telling me afterwards – I had put the caps in my pocket. We had to keep the caps and the dynamite separate. So I had put the caps in my shirt pocket. Somebody told me when it was all done – we were talking to somebody about it, I don't remember who, but they said, "Man, that is the most dangerous thing you probably ever will do is put caps in the pocket of your shirt because it's very easy to go off, those caps".
Sarah	What is a cap?
Marc	That's what detonates the dynamite.
Albert	Yeah, and if I'd have fallen or something or something would have hit that cap it could have blown my chest out of my body. We didn't know what we were doing.
Marc	No, we had no idea what we were doing. It's funny we didn't get blown up. (tuts) Kids… We didn't get any fish, I remember that.
Albert	No, no – no fish at all.
Marc	I remember that was a real pretty spot we had gone out to. Whose property is that?
Sarah	Albert, this is boiling now, is that what it should look like?
Albert	No, that's a little too high. I gotta turn it down. You need a real slow boil. Just a real small bubble every now and then.
Albert	It belongs to the Lores, Carl Lore's daddy–
Marc	Is he still living, Carl Lore?
Albert	No, he's deceased. He's been deceased for years.
	(Wilson, the youngest Savoy boy, comes in)
Wilson	Mom said we were eating at six, so I wanted to be here.
Marc	You're not gonna miss it.
Albert	I'm going to go ahead and cover it now. Now, this is what we have to fry, over here…
Sarah	So that's the belly of the fish?
Albert	Some of it, and some of its fillet, yeah…
Sarah	Is this all one fish?
Albert	No, this is two. This comes from the same place I usually fish, Intracoastal Canal. A friend of mine just caught that. That's the best place for me to fish because I like to fish catfish. We fish with throw lines. I tie my line to the bank and I back off. I have eight and ten hooks per line. We bait the hooks as we back off in a boat and then we drop a weight at the end. They fish all night. We go back to the camp and we cook and we eat supper and we sleep, then the next morning we run our lines and there's the fish!

FISH & SEAFOOD

Sarah	Where is Intracoastal Canal?
Albert	It's about eleven miles south of Kaplan and it runs coast-to-coast, California to the east side.
Sarah	Is that man-made?
Albert	Yes, it's man made. It's a good body of water. The water always moves in there. You got water from Vermillion Bay that comes in there from the east, and from the west you get water from White Lake or Lake Charles or Big Lake and those places always have catfish. That's how come we always have so much catfish. I've been fishing there for about thirty years.
Sarah	Where else do you go?
Albert	We used to go to Toledo Bin to fish. That's a good place. We don't fish catfish there, though. We used to fish Brim and Sac-au-lait *[which, Albert informed me, is the state fish of Louisiana]*. But they went ahead and stocked Toledo Bin with catfish and they tell me they got catfish in there big enough to swallow a man. I don't know how true that is, but they claim there's some big catfish.
Marc	The last time I went fishing with Albert, Sarah, we fished, we fished, we fished. We caught choupiques. Remember that, Albert? As fast as we could pull them out of the water we'd catch another one.
Albert	Yeah, that was just before *[Hurricane]* Audrey.
Marc	We were at my uncle's camp. We cleaned the fish. I was seventeen. How old were you then, Albert?
Albert	I was about fourteen.
Marc	We cleaned our fish and put them in a freezer and a few days later, Hurricane Audrey came and wiped out the camp. We found the freezer miles off in the marshes full of rotten food. So all the food was lost. I think that's the last time Albert and I went fishing. We opened up the freezer and it just exploded.
Albert	And I had begged Momma and them to bring that fish. I said, "We can't leave that fish!" They said we'd come back in a few days.
Marc	We worked like slaves. We were so proud of our choupiques.
Sarah	And you don't know what kind of fish a choupique is?
Marc	What is that, Albert, a mudfish?
Albert	Yeah, they call that a mudfish.
Marc	They consider that a trash fish, but if you want to have a fish that really fights on your line it's a choupique. Boy, those things can fight.
Albert	Oh, yeah. It's a fun fish to catch. We barbecued them already and they were pretty good.
Marc	They're cottony.
Wilson	Are y'all actually gonna fry fish or no?
Albert	Oh, yeah! And you smell that courtbouillon?
Wilson	Yep, that's my favourite.
Marc	My grandmother would make the courtbouillon with a white sauce. I've never eaten it. Tina was telling me she made one recently.

FISH & SEAFOOD

Albert	I've made that, yeah. It's good. You just do the same thing but without tomato sauce. I did it because the store at the camp was closed and we were stuck without tomato sauce. So I did it and it was good, but–
Marc	But not as good as–
Albert	No, I prefer it with just that little bit of tomato sauce. Sometimes we used to make tomato sauce. We still do sometimes, but we buy most of it. We make it, I guess, just to keep the, uh– But it's pretty good.

FISH & SEAFOOD

Aubergine Pirogue

SERVES 4

The classic stuffed, fried, baked aubergine. I read somewhere once that if there was a bible of Louisiana cooking, the first commandment would be "fry that sucker". Perhaps this isn't too far from the truth.

---

2 LARGE AUBERGINES, CUT IN HALF LENGTHWISE

2 COD FILLETS

JUICE OF 1 LEMON

30G (2 TBSP) BUTTER

1 TBSP OLIVE OIL

110G (4OZ) SMOKED SAUSAGE, CUT INTO VERY SMALL CUBES

1 LARGE ONION, MINCED

1/4 GREEN PEPPER, MINCED

1/4 RED PEPPER, MINCED

1 GARLIC CLOVE, MINCED

60ML (1/4 CUP) DRY WHITE WINE

250G (9OZ) CRAB MEAT

110G (4OZ) SMALL UNCOOKED PRAWNS, PEELED

60G (1 CUP) FRESH BREADCRUMBS

1 TSP FRESH PARSLEY, MINCED

1 SPRING ONION, FINELY SLICED

6 TBSP FLOUR

75G (3/4 CUP) PARMESAN CHEESE, GRATED

SALT

BLACK PEPPER

CAYENNE

VEGETABLE OIL FOR DEEP FRYING

Preheat the oven to 220°C (425°F).

Cut cross-hatches into the cut side of each aubergine half and place them cut-side-down on a greased baking sheet. Bake for 10 minutes, then turn them over and bake for 5 minutes more, or until they're tender. Remove from oven and let the aubergines cool for 10 minutes. Scrape out the tender pulp and reserve about half. Place the aubergine shells on a lightly greased baking sheet.

Reduce oven temperature to 180°C (350°F). Cut each cod fillet in half lengthwise so they're a similar size and shape to the aubergines, season them well, then drizzle with half of the lemon juice. Melt half of the butter in a large, non-stick frying pan over medium heat and fry the fish for 2 minutes on each side. Set the fish aside on a plate.

Add the olive oil to the pan, and when it's hot put in the sausage, onion, green and red peppers and garlic. Sauté for 5 minutes. Add the reserved aubergine pulp and the white wine and cook for another 10 minutes, stirring regularly. Stir in the crab meat and prawns, cook for a further minute then take the pan off the heat. Add the breadcrumbs, parsley and spring onions and stir gently to combine. Season to taste with salt, black pepper and cayenne.

Heat enough vegetable oil to deep fry the aubergines in a deep pan over medium-high heat.

Lay one piece of fried fish carefully in each aubergine shell, then cover it with about 6 tablespoons of the stuffing mixture to form a small mound in each. Put the flour on a large plate and roll each stuffed aubergine lightly in the flour. Deep fry them in batches for 5 minutes, or until golden brown all over, then drain them on paper towels.

Melt the remaining butter, and whisk it with a tablespoon of lemon juice. Drizzle this over the stuffed aubergines, then sprinkle them with Parmesan cheese. Bake for 10 minutes or until the prawns are cooked and the stuffing is piping hot.

Serve with French bread and a green salad.

FISH & SEAFOOD

Crayfish Etouffee

SERVES 4

Marc Savoy's recipe

```
50ML (3 1/2 TBSP) VEGETABLE OIL
450G (1LB) CRAYFISH TAILS
1/2 TBSP FLOUR
1/2 ONION, CHOPPED
1/4 GREEN PEPPER, CHOPPED
3 CLOVES GARLIC, MINCED
4 SPRING ONIONS, GREEN PARTS ONLY,
FINELY SLICED
2 TBSP PARSLEY, MINCED
15G (1 TBSP) BUTTER
125ML (1/2 CUP) TOMATO PASSATA
SALT
BLACK PEPPER
CAYENNE
```

Many people make crayfish etouffee with a roux, which makes it a much heavier meal. Dad likes to make it without, allowing the flavour of the crayfish to really dominate the dish. This is his recipe.

Heat the oil in a large, heavy frying pan over medium-high heat. Add the crayfish tails and season well with salt, black pepper and cayenne. Cook them, stirring frequently, for 10 minutes or until they reach a nicely-browned colour. Sprinkle over the flour and stir so it is thoroughly incoporated.

Add the onion, green pepper, garlic, spring onions, parsley and butter. Cook for 10 minutes, stirring frequently to stop it catching, then pour in the passata. Turn the heat down and simmer the etouffee gently for another 10 minutes.

Serve over steamed, long grain white rice.

FISH & SEAFOOD

SERVES 4

```
125ML (1/2 CUP) VEGETABLE OIL
30G (2 TBSP) BUTTER
75G (1/2 CUP) FLOUR
1 LARGE ONION, CHOPPED
1 LARGE GREEN PEPPER, CHOPPED
3 STALKS CELERY, CHOPPED (OPTIONAL)
4 CLOVES GARLIC, MINCED
350G (12OZ) CRAYFISH TAILS
(IF YOU CAN FIND THEM WITH THAT
WONDERFUL YELLOW FAT, LUCKY YOU!)
375ML (1 1/2 CUPS) STOCK (CRAYFISH,
SHRIMP, VEGETABLE, OR EVEN
CHICKEN) OR WATER
1 SMALL BUNCH SPRING ONIONS,
GREEN PARTS ONLY, SLICED
SALT
BLACK PEPPER
CAYENNE
```

Uncle Coonie's recipe

Start by making a roux. Heat the oil in a heavy pan over medium-high heat and add the butter. Mix in the flour and stir the roux continuously until it turns dark brown, about the colour of milk chocolate (be patient, this can take up to 30 minutes).

Carefully stir in the onion, green pepper, celery (or not) and garlic and cook for 8 minutes or until the vegetables are soft. Stir in the crayfish tails and cook for another 5 minutes, then pour in the stock or water, season with salt, black pepper and cayenne and simmer for 20 minutes.

Serve over steamed white rice, garnished with sliced spring onions.

FISH & SEAFOOD

Atchafalaya Special Fried Fish with Crayfish Etouffee Topping

SERVES 4

- 15G (1 TBSP) BUTTER
- 1 TBSP PEANUT OIL
- 5 TBSP FLOUR
- 1/2 ONION, FINELY CHOPPED
- 1/2 GREEN PEPPER, FINELY CHOPPED
- 4 LARGE TOMATOES, CHOPPED
- 450G (1LB) CRAYFISH TAILS
- 3 TBSP CORNMEAL
- 4 COD FILLETS
- 1 LEMON, CUT INTO 4 WEDGES
- 4 SPRING ONIONS, GREEN PARTS ONLY, SLICED
- 1/2 SMALL BUNCH OF PARSLEY, FINELY CHOPPED
- SALT
- BLACK PEPPER
- CAYENNE

VEGETABLE OIL FOR DEEP FRYING

Melt the butter in a large, heavy frying pan over medium heat. Add the peanut oil and 2 tablespoons of flour and cook until you have a tan roux, stirring all the while. When it's a good colour, carefully stir in the onion, green pepper and tomatoes and season well with salt, black pepper and cayenne. Cook for 12 minutes until the onions have softened, then add the crayfish tails and cook for another 10 minutes. Reduce heat to very low to keep the etouffee warm.

Heat vegetable oil to a depth of 5cm in a deep, heavy pan. While it's heating, mix the remaining 3 tablespoons of flour and cornmeal together and season with salt, black pepper and plenty of cayenne. Dredge each fish fillet in the seasoned flour, and place immediately in the hot oil. Fry for 2 minutes per side, then remove to a plate of paper towels to drain –put the plate in a warm oven while you get on with the other fillets so the fish doesn't get cold.

Squeeze a lemon quarter over each fish fillet and top with a quarter of the crayfish etouffee, spring onions and chopped parsley.

Serve with corn macque choux (see page 43) or steamed, long grain white rice.

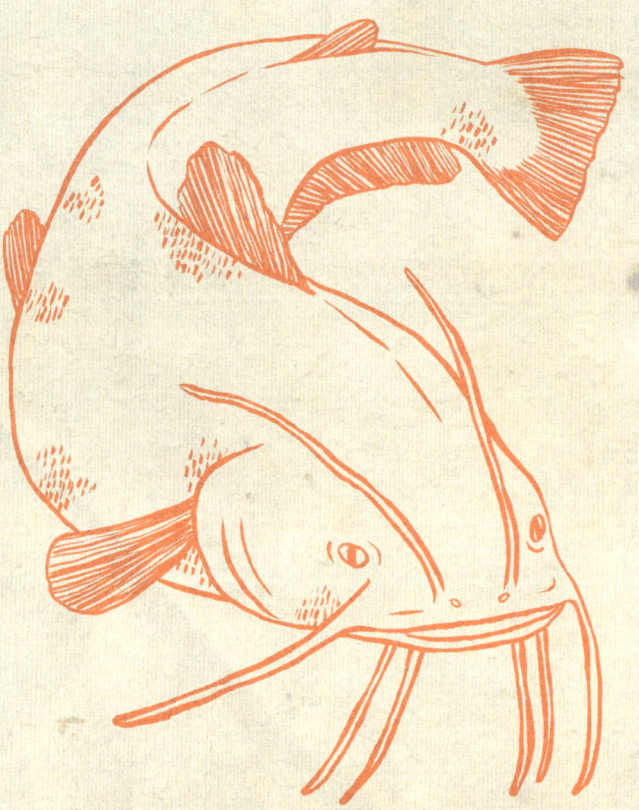

FISH & SEAFOOD

Crayfish Pie

SERVES 8-10

Sarah Savoy & the Francadians' *accordionist David and I were talking about food one night after a gig and he told me that Crayfish Pie never actually existed before Hank Williams wrote "Jambalaya". He said people kept coming down to Louisiana and demanding Crayfish Pie, but no one had ever heard of it, so they decided to invent one. I don't know if that's true or not, but I like the story.*

Here's my recipe for this mysterious dish, which I love to bring to parties. I have a cookie cutter in the shape of a crayfish that I like to use to cut out pastry decorations to stick on the top of the pie. It's fine to use shop-bought shortcrust pastry if you don't want to make it.

```
1 TBSP BUTTER
1 MEDIUM ONION, FINELY CHOPPED
1/2 GREEN PEPPER, FINELY CHOPPED
2 MEDIUM TOMATOES, PEELED AND
CHOPPED
600G (1LB 5OZ) CRAYFISH TAILS
2 TBSP PLAIN FLOUR
140G (1 CUP) CHEDDAR OR MIMOLETTE
CHEESE, GRATED
2 X QUANTITY PASTRY (SEE P.116 BUT
OMIT THE SUGAR) OR 500G (1LB)
SHOP-BOUGHT PASTRY
1 EGG, BEATEN
SALT
BLACK PEPPER
CAYENNE

23CM PIE DISH
```

Melt the butter in a large heavy pan over medium heat. Add the onions, green pepper and tomatoes and sauté them for 8 minutes or until the onions are soft. Add the crayfish tails and cook for a couple of minutes, then taste and season with salt, black pepper and cayenne. Drain off any excess liquid from the pan. Mix the flour with 5 tablespoons of water in a small cup and stir this into the crayfish. Cook gently for 2 minutes, then stir in the grated cheese and remove from the heat. Let it cool at least 30 minutes.

Preheat the oven to 180°C (350°F). Roll out half of your pastry and use it to line the pie dish. Prick all over with a fork, then fill with the cooled crayfish mixture. Brush the lip of the pastry with beaten egg, then roll out the remaining dough and cover the pie, trimming and crimping the edges with a fork. Pierce the top to let any steam escape and brush with whatever beaten egg you have left.

Bake the pie for 40 minutes until it is golden brown. Serve hot with sliced tomatoes and coleslaw.

FISH & SEAFOOD

Crayfish Enchiladas

SERVES 4-6

- 30G (2 TBSP) BUTTER
- 3 LARGE TOMATOES
- 1 GREEN CHILLI, SEEDS REMOVED, MINCED
- 1 1/2 TBSP PLAIN FLOUR
- 1 1/2 TBSP PEANUT OIL
- 1/2 ONION, FINELY CHOPPED
- 1/2 GREEN PEPPER, FINELY CHOPPED
- 2 CLOVES GARLIC, MINCED
- 450G (1LB) CRAYFISH TAILS
- 100G (2/3 CUP) CHEDDAR OR MIMOLETTE CHEESE, GRATED
- 75G (3/4 CUP) STEAMED, LONG GRAIN WHITE RICE
- 6 LARGE FLOUR TORTILLAS
- 50ML (3 HEAPED TBSP) SOUR CREAM
- 3 SPRING ONIONS, GREEN PARTS ONLY, THINLY SLICED
- 3 SPRIGS OF PARSLEY, FINELY CHOPPED
- SALT
- BLACK PEPPER
- CAYENNE

Preheat oven to 200°C (400°F).

Melt the butter in a small pan over medium-high heat. Peel, seed and chop 2 of the tomatoes and add to the pan, cooking for 10 minutes until they have a jammy consistency. Use a hand mixer or a potato masher to reduce to a pulp, then add 3 tablespoons of water and the minced chilli. Simmer gently for 10 minutes then take the pan off the heat.

In a large, heavy pan over medium heat, cook the flour in the peanut oil to make a tan roux, stirring all the time. Chop the remaining tomato, and carefully stir it in along with the onion, green pepper and garlic (it will splutter and spit). Continue cooking until the vegetables are very soft (about 8 minutes). Add the crayfish tails and season well with salt, black pepper and cayenne. Cook for 2 minutes. Add about two-thirds of the grated cheese and cook for 2 more minutes, then remove from the heat and mix in the cooked rice. Taste and season again if it needs it.

Butter a deep baking dish. Fill each tortilla with approximately 6 tablespoons of the crayfish stuffing, then fold up the ends and roll it into a tube (so that the enchiladas have closed ends and the filling won't leak out). Line the enchiladas up snugly in the baking dish. Pour the tomato and chilli sauce over them, spread sour cream evenly over the top, and then sprinkle with the remaining cheese, spring onions and parsley.

Bake for 15 minutes or until the cheese melts and everything is starting to bubble.

Serve with Mexican cornbread and more sour cream.

FISH & SEAFOOD

Crayfish Fettuccine

SERVES 4

No one in my family ever made this, but I had plenty of it at friends' homes. This is an excellent example of the difference between Cajun and Creole cooking. Because the Creoles were wealthy aristocrats, many had brought their own chefs with them to Louisiana from France, Spain, and Italy. Also, with New Orleans being a port city, foreign ingredients like pasta were available to them to come up with dishes like this one.

I'm guessing it's too rich to be something either of my parents would ever want to cook, but I'm a big fan of butter and cream! Feel free to use small or medium prawns instead of crayfish if you prefer.

350G (12OZ) CRAYFISH TAILS
225G (8OZ) FETTUCCINE
100G (7 TBSP) BUTTER
1 ONION, CHOPPED
1/2 GREEN PEPPER, CHOPPED
1 1/2 TBSP PLAIN FLOUR
140G (1 CUP) CHEDDAR OR MIMOLETTE CHEESE, GRATED
1 RED CHILLI, MINCED
125ML (1/2 CUP) DOUBLE CREAM
1 GARLIC CLOVE, FINELY CHOPPED
1 1/2 TBSP PARSLEY, FINELY CHOPPED
50G (1/2 CUP) PARMESAN CHEESE, GRATED
SALT
BLACK PEPPER
CAYENNE

Preheat the oven to 180°C (350°F).

Put the crayfish tails into a bowl and season them well with salt, black pepper and cayenne.

Bring a large pan of water to the boil and cook the fettuccine according to the package directions. Leave to drain in a colander.

Melt the butter in a large pan over medium heat. Sauté the onion and green pepper for 5 minutes, then sprinkle over the flour and mix it in thoroughly. Cover the pan, and sweat for 15 minutes, stirring frequently. Add the Cheddar cheese, chilli, cream and garlic and cook gently for 5 minutes, then stir in the crayfish tails and parsley and cook for 5 minutes more.

Toss the drained fettuccine and the crayfish sauce together. Check the seasoning and adjust as necessary, then pile everything into a deep baking dish. Sprinkle with Parmesan cheese and bake for 15–20 minutes until everything is hot and bubbling and the cheese has begun to brown.

FISH & SEAFOOD

Crab Cakes Savoy

SERVES 6

FOR THE CRAB CAKES
- 45G (3 TBSP) BUTTER
- 1 SMALL YELLOW ONION, MINCED
- 1/2 RED PEPPER, MINCED
- 2 GARLIC CLOVES, MINCED
- 120G (2 CUPS) BREADCRUMBS
- 1/4 TSP DRIED THYME
- 1/4 TSP CELERY SALT
- 1/4 TSP DRIED PARSNIPS (OPTIONAL, BUT GREAT IF YOU CAN FIND THEM)
- 1 SMALL BUNCH OF SPRING ONIONS, GREEN PARTS ONLY, THINLY SLICED
- 3 TBSP MAYONNAISE
- 1 TBSP SOUR CREAM
- 1 EGG, BEATEN
- 2 TBSP FRESH PARSLEY, MINCED
- 1 TSP WORCESTERSHIRE SAUCE
- 2 TSP LEMON JUICE
- 2 TBSP MILK
- 1 TSP DIJON MUSTARD
- 2 DASHES OF HOT SAUCE
- 350G (12OZ) WHITE LUMP CRAB MEAT
- SALT
- BLACK PEPPER
- CAYENNE

FOR THE SAUCE
- 200G (3/4 CUP & 2 TBSP) BUTTER
- 3 TBSP DRY WHITE WINE
- 1/2 TSP LEMON JUICE
- 100G (3 1/2 OZ) WHITE LUMP CRAB MEAT

Pete Stevens, drummer of the rockin' Louisiana band **Filé**, first turned me on to crab cakes when he gave me his own recipe for Crab Cakes Provençale, accompanied by a small bag of Provençale seasoning. This was back when I was working at **Randol's** in Lafayette, where live bands were playing every night for diners enjoying some of the best seafood in Louisiana and a local television crew was filming the bands and dancers one night a week. Since then, I've searched out just about every crab cake and crab cake recipe I could find and come up with my own recipe. Pete's is still one of the best, but you'll have to ask him for it!

Crab cakes make an excellent brunch or lunch. I like to serve these on a thick slice of tomato or a polenta cake in a little pool of sauce for brunch, or on a bed of crab corn maque choux and lettuce for lunch. Some people also like a Louisiana Benedict Arnold, which features a poached egg on a crab cake on an English muffin, dripping with hollandaise sauce. Whichever way you choose to serve them, I hope you and your family and friends will love them.

Melt 15g (1 tbsp) of butter in a large pan over medium-high heat. Add onion, red pepper and garlic and sauté for 5 minutes. Remove the pan from the heat.

Put the breadcrumbs in a large bowl and mix in the thyme, celery salt and dried parsnips. Season with salt, black pepper and cayenne. Cut the remaining butter into the breadcrumbs with a knife and then stir in the spring onions, mayonnaise, sour cream, beaten egg, fresh parsley, Worcestershire sauce, lemon juice, milk, mustard and hot sauce. Mix in the sautéed vegetables and taste and adjust for seasonings. Gently fold in the crab meat with a spatula (taking care not to break it up too much) until everything is well mixed.

Line a baking tray with baking parchment. Using your hands, gently form 12 patties from the crab mixture, about 2 cm thick and 4 cm in diameter. Place the crab cakes on the lined tray and put in the fridge to firm up for about 1½ hours.

Heat the grill to its highest setting. Put the crab cakes on their baking tray under the grill for 3-4 minutes on each side, until they're lightly browned and hot in the middle. Be very careful when you turn them as they can be a little fragile.

Now, get on with the sauce. Melt the butter in a small pan and pour it into a heavy bowl or mug. With a hand mixer running, slowly pour in the wine and lemon juice and keep mixing the sauce until it emulsifies. Return to the pan on a low heat, and crumble in the crab meat with your fingers, breaking it up slightly. Heat the sauce through.

You've now got 2 options... For brunch: pour a small pool of sauce onto each plate. Set a thick slice of tomato in the middle, top with a crab cake and drizzle sparingly with another teaspoon of sauce. Garnish with a sprig of parsley or dill.

For lunch: arrange a layer of lettuce leaves on each plate. Put a small bed of crab corn macque choux (see page 43) on top, and put a crab cake on top of that. Drizzle it with about 2 tablespoons of sauce and garnish with some lemon zest and a sprig of parsley or dill.

FISH & SEAFOOD

Oysters Rockefeller

SERVES 4

Chez Francois, a seafood market in Lafayette, Louisiana, once had a special on oysters—100 pounds of oysters in their shells for $30. I was driving by, saw the sign, and decided to buy 100 pounds of oysters. Once the man loaded them into the trunk of my car in a big sack, covering the trunk upholstery with plastic garbage bags, I drove home to the house I was renting. On the way there I started thinking, "One hundred pounds of oysters looks like a lot. I don't even know how to cook oysters! Can I eat these raw? How can I bake them like they do in restaurants? Spinach? Cheese? How many people does it take to eat a hundred pounds of oysters? How the heck do you shuck an oyster? What am I going to do??" I got home and called some friends over. They dragged the sack of oysters out of my car and dumped it on the gravel parking lot.

One friend suggested putting them on the barbecue pit, cooking them that way until they popped open, then eating them with butter and hot sauce (they were delicious like this, by the way). His friend, who was with him, said he knew how to shuck oysters. Yay! I broke out a cookbook by Emeril Lagasse, king of New Orleans cuisine and found at least 10 oyster recipes. I was set! It was time to call more friends and go to the grocery store.

This is one of the recipes I used from Emeril's cookbook. It may have changed over the years, but I owe Emeril a huge favour for saving me after that insane impulse buy. Everything he does is amazing. Order his cookbooks from your local bookstore to make oysters exactly his way and amaze your friends.

Oh, and the end of the story? We never did finish the oysters that night, but the next day I brought all the leftovers out to my dad's Saturday morning jam session and they were gone in no time. Feeding friends and family is what it's all about.

Ingredients:
- 1 BAG OF ROCK SALT
- 8 SLICES STREAKY BACON, COOKED AND CRUMBLED
- 3 TBSP CELERY LEAVES, CHOPPED
- 3 TBSP CHERVIL, CHOPPED
- 6 SPRING ONIONS, GREEN PARTS ONLY, FINELY CHOPPED
- 1 SMALL BUNCH OF PARSLEY, CHOPPED
- 90G (1 1/2 CUPS) SPINACH, VERY FINELY CHOPPED
- JUICE OF 2 LEMONS
- 30G (1/2 CUP) BREADCRUMBS
- 4 TBSP OLIVE OIL
- 24 OYSTERS ON THE HALF SHELL, DRAINED, SAND REMOVED
- 110G (1/2 CUP) BUTTER
- SALT
- BLACK PEPPER
- CAYENNE

Preheat the oven to 190°C (375°F). Pour a 2 cm layer of rock salt into a baking dish large enough to fit all the oysters.

Combine the bacon, celery, chervil, spring onion, parsley, and spinach in a large mixing bowl. Season with salt and black pepper and sprinkle with the lemon juice.

In another bowl, stir together the breadcrumbs and olive oil and season well with salt, black pepper and cayenne.

Push the oysters into the rock salt to anchor them. Cover each one with a pile of bacon/greens stuffing, and then with a layer of breadcrumbs. Put a small knob of butter (about ¼ tsp) on top of each one, and bake for 10–15 minutes until lightly browned.

Serve directly from the baking dish, with French bread and spinach salad.

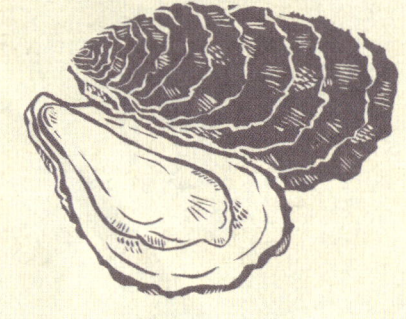

FISH & SEAFOOD

Oysters Savoy

SERVES 4

Having bought 100 pounds of oysters, I had enough to experiment with, and this was one of the experiments that turned out the best. It was a matter of tossing together what was in the refrigerator and I find that's almost always a lucky way to cook.

- 1 BAG OF ROCK SALT
- 450G (1LB) SMOKED PORK SAUSAGE, DICED
- 75G (1/3 CUP) PARSLEY, FINELY CHOPPED
- 1/2 RED PEPPER, FINELY CHOPPED
- 3 GARLIC CLOVES, FINELY CHOPPED
- JUICE OF 1 LEMON
- 30G (1/2 CUP) BREADCRUMBS
- 4 TBSP OLIVE OIL
- 1/2 TSP DRIED BASIL
- 100G (1 CUP) PARMESAN CHEESE, GRATED
- 24 OYSTERS ON THE HALF SHELL, DRAINED, SAND REMOVED
- 110G (1/2 CUP) BUTTER
- SALT
- BLACK PEPPER
- CAYENNE

Preheat the oven to 190°C (375°F).

Pour a 2 cm layer of rock salt into a large baking dish.

Combine the sausage, parsley, red pepper and garlic in a large mixing bowl. Season with salt and black pepper and sprinkle with lemon juice.

In another bowl, stir together the breadcrumbs, Parmesan and olive oil and season well with basil, salt, black pepper and cayenne.

Push the oysters into the rock salt to anchor them. Cover each one with a layer of the sausage mixture, and then a layer of the seasoned breadcrumbs. Put a knob of butter (about ¼ tsp) on top of each and bake them for 10-15 minutes or until lightly browned.

Serve directly from the baking dish with French bread and spinach salad.

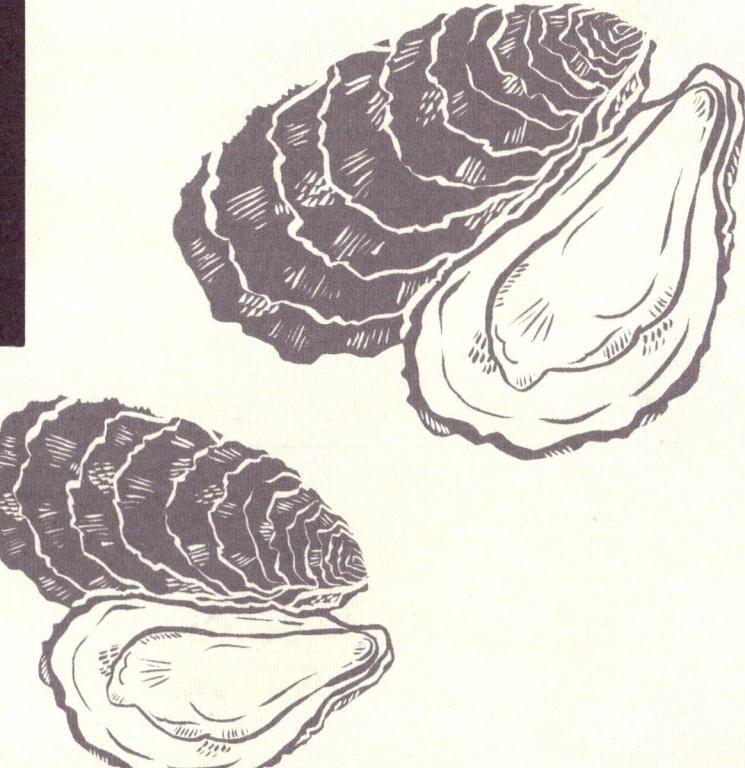

FISH & SEAFOOD

Beer Batter & PoBoys

So let's get to some of those wonderfully fattening fried foods! Beer batter is where it's at for fish fillets, crayfish tails, prawns, oysters, chicken strips, onion rings, okra, green tomato slices, jalapeños – even sliced cucumber pickles! Serve the fried stuff next to more fried stuff if you want to do it the most common Louisiana-diner style. Personally, I love a big salad topped with a few large, fried prawns, and few things please me more than a lightly-fried oyster PoBoy.

Deep frying really doesn't deserve the bad reputation it has. Use polyunsaturated vegetable oil, keep the oil clean, and do not use it more than ten times. Fry in small batches so as not to radically lower the temperature of the oil when the food is added. If the oil is hot enough (190°C/375°F, usually), and you drain the fried meat or vegetable on paper towels briefly before serving, the end product is actually fairly light.

Beer Batter

150ML (2/3 CUP) LIGHT BEER

2 EGGS

120G (3/4 CUP) FINE CORNMEAL

SALT

BLACK PEPPER

CAYENNE

Whisk together the beer and eggs in one bowl, and sift the cornmeal into another. Season the cornmeal well with salt, black pepper and cayenne.

Dip whatever you're frying into the egg mixture, then the cornmeal, and then repeat. Deep fry immediately in hot oil until golden.

Another popular method of frying, especially for oysters, scallops, fish and prawns, is to simply roll the seafood in seasoned cornflour before sliding it into the hot oil.

PoBoys

Somehow Louisiana got to be known for the "poor-boy" sandwich as well. A PoBoy, however, is nothing more than a sub or hoagie sandwich that you'd find anywhere else. There are only two differences: it's served on crusty French bread, and Cajuns may have gotten a little more inventive with the fillings…

You've got your basics, like ham and cheese, club, bacon-lettuce-tomato and so on, and the regular condiments like mayo and a bit of wholegrain mustard, and the filler vegetables are always there (lettuce, tomato, and thinly sliced red onion, if you like it), but you can stuff your individual-sized baguette with everything you like. Some favourites include the following:

FISH & SEAFOOD

Prawns

Fried, boiled, or grilled

Fried oysters

I fry mine in very hot oil for only about 30 seconds

Chicken

the breast fillets can be barbecued, deep fried, pan fried or baked with garlic and Creole seasoning, or cooked any way you like your chicken prepared.

Pulled-Pork

Pulled-pork is a pork roast cooked in a slow-cooker (use the barbecue sauce recipe to season it as it cooks) until tender enough to pull apart with a fork. The sauce can replace the usual condiments. Top with coleslaw for a nice crunch.

Roast Beef

Replace the mustard with a bit of horseradish.

These are just a few of the most popular fillings in Louisiana. Many PoBoy kitchens also serve pizza PoBoys, hamburger PoBoys, cheeseburger PoBoys, etc. Try your own ideas and you'll always have a tasty, filling lunch.

FISH & SEAFOOD

Soft Ginger Br[ead]

1 cup sugar
1/2 " syrup
1/2 " shortening
1/2 teaspoon g[inger]
1 " cinnamon
1 " soda di[ssolved in]
boiling water
2½ cups flour
2 eggs beaten
before cooking

co[...]
Plea[...]

Fig Drop Cookies

1 cup shortening
1½ cup ~~syrup~~ sugar
2 eggs
1 cup syrup
4 " flour
2 teaspoon soda
1 " cinnamon
1 " vanilla flavo[r]
2 cups figs
1 " nuts

Pauline's

written by Mama — Mabel B. Savoy

Syrup Cake

1 egg
½ cup sugar
⅓ cup lard
1 cup syrup
½ cup boiling water
2 teaspoon ginger
2 teaspoon cinnamon
1 teaspoon soda
2½ cup flour
1 cup raisins
[...]
[...]

written by Mama — Mabel B. Savoy

Desserts

Pastry	P.116
Pecan Pie	P.117
Sweet Potato Pie	P.118
Buttermilk Pie	P.119
Rhubarb Pie	P.120
Mom Mabel's Banana Nut Cake	P.122
Pineapple Upside-Down Cake	P.124
Gâteau de Sirop (Syrup Cake)	P.125
King Cake	P.126
Bourbon Bread Pudding	P.128
Pecan Crêpes	P.129
Candied Sweet Potatoes	P.130
Bananas Foster	P.131
Mom Mabel's Fig Drop Cookies	P.132
Oreilles de Cochons (Pig's Ears)	P.133
Pecan Pralines	P.134
Boules Rouges	P.135

Pastry

Pretty much everyone I know has their own pastry recipe, and they are all wildly different. I change mine a little depending on what I'm going to use it for, but here is a standard, go-to pastry recipe you can use for anything. If you're making a savoury pie, just leave out the sugar. If you prefer store-bought pastry, nothing wrong with that. Only I'm often too lazy to get dressed and go to the store when I feel like making a pie, and, anyway, I really do think that homemade pastry tastes better no matter what you put in it.

This recipe makes enough to line a 23–25cm pie dish. If you're making a pie with a top (like the rhubarb pie on page 120), just double up the quantities.

190G (1 1/4 CUPS) PLAIN FLOUR
PINCH OF SALT
1 TBSP SUGAR (OMIT FOR A SAVOURY PIE)
110G (1/2 CUP) UNSALTED BUTTER, CHILLED, CUT INTO SMALL CUBES
3–4 TBSP ICED WATER

Sift the flour, salt and sugar (if using) together in a large mixing bowl. Using two knives or a pastry cutter, cut the butter into the flour mixture until there are no pieces of fat left larger than a pea. Using the blade of a rubber spatula, mix in 3 tablespoons of iced water and keep pressing the dough down in a folding motion until it comes together. If it doesn't stick, gradually add another tablespoon of iced water until it does.

Divide the pastry into 2 balls and flatten them into 10cm rounds. Dust the rounds lightly with flour, wrap them in cling film, and refrigerate for at least 30 minutes before rolling out (you can also leave them for up to 2 days in the fridge). Let the pastry sit at room temperature for 5 minutes before you use it.

DESSERTS

Pecan Pie

SERVES 8

Pecan pie is probably perfect just about any time of year, but my favourite time to eat it is in the autumn, when the days are getting shorter and the weather is clear and sunny, but cool with a chilly breeze. Something about the way autumn light colours everything makes food taste differently somehow, but maybe that's just because I always feel different about everything in the autumn. Or it could be just the memory of picking pecans from the ground along the gravel road to our house with Dad, him always in his red and black checkered flannel shirt.

```
2 EGGS
250ML (1 CUP) MAPLE SYRUP
2 TBSP GRANULATED SUGAR
2 TBSP BROWN SUGAR
1 TBSP FLOUR
1/4 TSP SALT
1 TSP VANILLA EXTRACT
1 QUANTITY PASTRY (SEE PAGE 116)
OR 250G (1/2 LB) SHOP-BOUGHT
300G (2 CUPS) WHOLE PECANS,
SHELLED AND PICKED THROUGH

23CM PIE DISH
```

Preheat the oven to 190°C (375°F).

Beat the eggs in a mixing bowl and add the maple syrup, white and brown sugar, flour, salt and vanilla extract. Mix well with a fork.

Roll out the pastry and line your pie dish. Trim and crimp the edges, and prick some holes in the base with a fork. Put in most of the pecans, reserving about 20 unbroken ones for the top, then pour over the egg mixture. Top with the reserved pecans.

Bake for 40-50 minutes or until the filling is set. If the pastry looks like it's burning, cover the pie loosely with foil towards the end of the cooking time.

Leave to cool for at least 30 minutes (or else the filling won't set and it will run everywhere. But then again, if you just wanna eat it with a spoon...).

DESSERTS

Sweet Potato Pie

SERVES 8

I can't imagine how Mom ever got me to try a pie made from a potato, sweet or not. I probably thought it was pumpkin because I'm sure I wouldn't have tried this as a kid if I knew what it was. I now prefer it to pumpkin. It's another one of those cool-weather pies, spicy and creamy and absolutely comforting.

- 450G (1LB) SWEET POTATOES
- 110G (1/2 CUP) BUTTER, SOFTENED
- 225G (1 CUP) WHITE SUGAR
- 125ML (1/2 CUP) MILK
- 2 EGGS, LIGHTLY BEATEN
- 1/4 TSP NUTMEG, FRESHLY GRATED
- 1/2 TSP GROUND CINNAMON
- DASH OF ALLSPICE
- 1 TSP VANILLA EXTRACT
- 1 QUANTITY PASTRY (SEE P.116) OR 250G (1/2 LB) SHOP-BOUGHT

23CM PIE DISH

Preheat the oven to 170°C (325°F).

Peel the sweet potatoes and cut into chunks, then boil them until tender. Drain, and leave to cool a moment.

In a large bowl, mash the sweet potato with a fork or potato masher. Using a hand mixer, add the butter and process until it's fully incorporated. Stir in the sugar, milk, eggs, nutmeg, cinnamon, allspice and vanilla extract and mix until you have a smooth batter.

Roll out the pastry and line your pie dish. Trim and crimp the edges, and make some holes in the base with a fork. Pour in the filling.

Bake the pie for 50-60 minutes or until a knife inserted in the centre comes out clean. The pie will rise as it bakes, but it will settle again as it cools.

Serve at room temperature or chilled.

DESSERTS

Buttermilk Pie

SERVES 8

This is one of the fastest, easiest pies to make that I know of, and it is so delicious any time of year. My dad can't help himself – every time I make a buttermilk pie he's waiting by the stove with a spoon in hand to grab a piece before the buttermilk custard is even cooled and set. You can also flavour it with lime or tangerine zest instead of the lemon if that's what you have to hand or prefer.

```
340G (1 1/2 CUPS) UNREFINED
CASTER SUGAR

1 TBSP PLAIN FLOUR

1 TBSP GRATED LEMON ZEST

4 LARGE EGGS, LIGHTLY BEATEN

250ML (1 CUP) BUTTERMILK

110G (1/2 CUP) BUTTER, SOFTENED

1 QUANTITY PASTRY (SEE P.116) OR
250G (1/2 LB) SHOP-BOUGHT

23CM PIE DISH
```

Preheat the oven to 180°C (350°F).

Combine the sugar, flour and lemon zest in a large bowl. Beat in the eggs, then the buttermilk, and finally the butter, and keep beating until everything is thoroughly combined.

Roll out the pastry and use it to line your pie dish, pricking some holes in the bottom with a fork. Trim and crimp the edges, then pour in the buttermilk batter. Bake for about 25 minutes, or until the top is lightly browned and the centre has set.

Let the pie cool for 30 minutes, then refrigerate it for at least an hour before serving.

DESSERTS

Rhubarb Pie

SERVES 8

Our cousin, Carolyn LaFleur, taught me to make this when I was a teenager. She really inspired a lot of my cooking back then. I loved visiting her in her beautiful Acadian-style family home (where some of our ancestors are buried just behind the house in a little shed to protect their graves), hearing her stories about growing up as one of my dad's neighbourhood playmates, and cooking with her. I like to keep the rhubarb in this just a little tart, and then eat the pie warm with a side of vanilla ice cream. Also, to me, this is a pie that just has to have a lattice top crust, like apple pie. A lot of people, my mom included, prefer that the rhubarb be mixed with fresh strawberries, but I like it just like this.

2 x quantity pastry (see p. 116) or 500g (1lb) shop-bought

280g (1 1/2 cups) sugar

110g (scant 1/2 cup) plain flour

8 stalks fresh rhubarb, cut into 2cm slices

15g (1 tbsp) butter

1 egg white

1 tbsp milk

23cm pie dish

Preheat your oven to 220°C (425°F). Roll out half of the pastry and line your pie dish, pricking holes with a fork in the base.

Mix the sugar and flour together in a bowl, and put about a third of this mixture in a layer on top of the pastry. Pile the rhubarb evenly on top, then cover it with the remaining sugar/flour mixture. Put little knobs of butter all over.

Roll out the rest of the pastry, and cut it into long strips. Using water to join the ends, make a lattice over the top of the pie. Beat the egg white and milk together in a small bowl and brush this over the pastry lattice.

Bake for 15 minutes on the bottom rack of the oven, then reduce the oven temperature to 175°C (340°F) and bake the pie for 45 minutes more. You might need to cover it loosely with foil towards the end of the cooking time to stop the pastry from burning.

Serve warm with ice cream!

DESSERTS

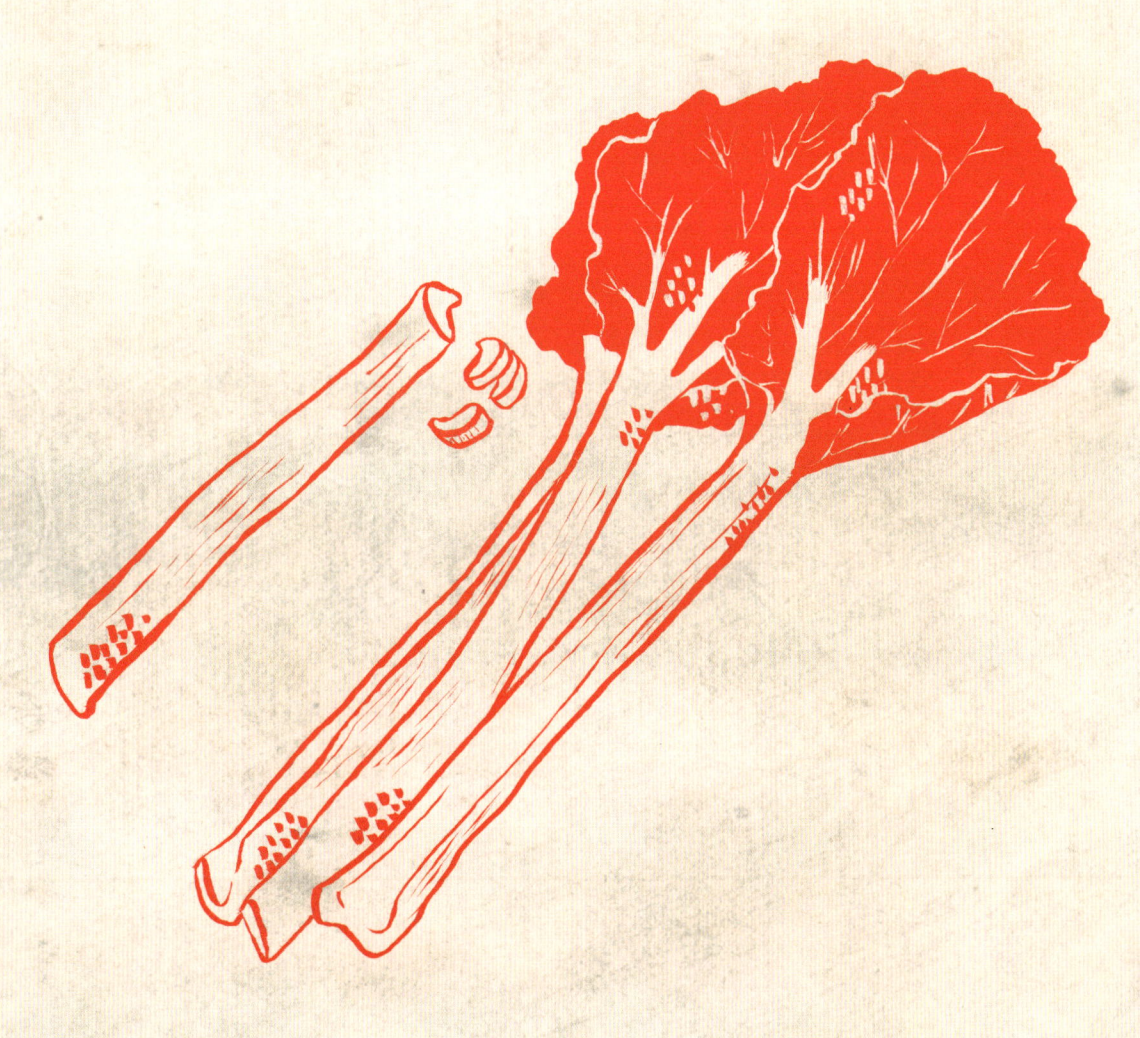

Mom Mabel's Banana Nut Cake   SERVES 10

The hand-written recipe pictured here was written by my paternal grandmother, Mabel Billadeaux Savoy. Mom gave me a book of recipes by Mabel and my maternal great-grandmother, Verna Jackson Chappell, and the first thing I noticed was that they had surprisingly similar penmanship. Next, I noticed that Mabel almost always wrote down only the ingredients for a recipe, meaning that she was cooking the rest by instinct and expected others to do the same. Verna, on the other hand, had carefully copied down both lists of ingredients and instructions for cooking or baking. She also had recipes cut out from magazines and pasted onto index cards in her recipe box. "Mom Mabel" had written her recipes on notepaper, either plain or from companies like "Olin Agricultural Division" and "Bostic Concrete Co., Inc.", often including the names of the friend who had given her the recipe.

I remember both women well. I was about 5 when Mom Mabel died, followed soon by her husband, "Pop", Joel Angelas Savoy, my first brother's namesake. I spent most of my mornings at their home when my mom was working on her book and my dad was at his store. I'd talk to Mom Mabel and she'd sew me the most amazing dresses, hand-smocked and carrying a little tag inside the back of the neck that read, "Made with love by Mom". She'd often take me grocery shopping, and then, when we got home, she'd prepare lunch and give me peach nectar to drink from the Sesame Street mug she had bought for me. While the food cooked, we'd watch The Price is Right together. She had a crush on Bob Barker, the show's host then. I'd sit in my little rocking chair next to a table on which sat a stuffed quail and a fringed lamp in a rose-coloured globe. Along with the crowd on television, Mom Mabel would yell, "Come on Down!" and laugh her full, warm, wild laugh. Pop would be out working in his garden with his dog all morning and would come in for lunch around noon. Lunches were always a delicious stewed meat, like a pot roast, with the gravy poured over rice, and a big plate of homegrown sliced tomatoes and cucumbers, drizzled with white vinegar and sprinkled with salt, black pepper and cayenne. My favourite part was the little bits of meat drippings that would stick to the pot. After lunch, I was supposed to nap until my dad came to pick me up. I was almost always in trouble because, instead of napping, I built forts from the sofa cushions.

We called Verna "Grandma Verna" like Mom did, even though she was our great-grandmother. (I have always called my grandmother "Lalla" because I couldn't say "Millie" when she was trying to teach me her name. To this day, Joel, Wilson, Gabie and I all still call her "Lalla".) Verna lived with her husband, Charlie Chappell, in Virginia. Their house, "Milbeth", was named after their two daughters, Mildred and Beth. There was a lake with a beaver dam next to the house and a huge expanse of soft, grassy land where we ran around, played croquet, swung in the hammock and ate our lunches. It seems Grandma Verna was always in the kitchen, playing dominoes or Old Maid with me while she cooked. She was a soft-spoken, Methodist lady from a half-English family. She had attended college and worked as a secretary for a long time, all during the early 1900's. She would read us stories and Grandpa Charlie would swing me in the hammock outside and sing me "You Are My Sunshine". As refined and gentle as both of them were, they somehow managed to handle the loud, wild Savoy children quite delicately and successfully.

DESSERTS

CAKE INGREDIENTS

- 150G (1 CUP) SHELLED PECANS
- 2 EGGS
- 115G (1/2 CUP) BUTTER
- 340G (1 1/2 CUPS) GRANULATED SUGAR
- 4 TBSP BUTTERMILK (OR MIX 4 TBSP WHOLE MILK WITH A DROP OF WHITE VINEGAR)
- 225G (1 1/2 CUP) PLAIN FLOUR
- 1 TSP BICARBONATE OF SODA
- PINCH OF SALT
- 3 SMALL BANANAS
- 1/2 TSP VANILLA EXTRACT

ICING INGREDIENTS

- 225G (1 CUP) BUTTER
- 125G (1 CUP) ICING SUGAR
- 1 SMALL BANANA
- 50G (1/3 CUP) SHELLED PECANS, TOASTED AND GROUND

A HANDFUL OF PECAN HALVES TO DECORATE

2 X 23CM ROUND CAKE TINS

Preheat the oven to 180°C (350°F). Grease and flour your cake tins.

While the oven is heating up, put all 200g (1 1/3 cups) of the pecans on a baking tray and put them in to toast. Take them out when you start to smell them – after about 5 minutes – and keep a close eye on them so they don't scorch. Put the nuts in a food processor and pulse them until they're quite finely ground. Set aside 50g (1/3 cup) to use in the icing.

Cream the eggs, butter and sugar together with a hand mixer until light and mousse-y. Fold in the buttermilk, flour, bicarbonate of soda and a pinch of salt.

In another bowl, mash 3 of the bananas well with a potato masher until you have a smooth purée. Add the vanilla extract and carefully fold the mixture into the cake batter. Finally, fold in the ground pecans.

Pour and scrape the batter into your cake tins and bake for 15–20 minutes, or until a toothpick inserted into the middle of the cake comes out clean. Leave the cakes to cool in their tins on a wire rack for 20 minutes.

To make the icing, melt the butter in a large saucepan. Add the icing sugar and stir until completely incorporated. Mash the remaining banana until it's smooth and add it in, then add the reserved ground pecans.

Put one of the cakes on a serving plate and spread with half of the icing. Put the second cake on top and spread with the remaining icing, then decorate with pecan halves.

Delicious.

DESSERTS

Pineapple Upside-Down Cake

SERVES 10

My great aunt Myrtle Riley, grandmother of Steve Riley (of **Steve Riley & the Mamou Playboys**), was famous in our family for the wild sense of humour that she shared with her sister, my grandmother, and for the desserts she brought to any family gathering. She would always bring in some kind of very sweet cake on a plate, covered with toothpicks holding the plastic wrap off the surface, and announce (unapologetically and with a mischievous grin), "It's not how it looks, but how it tastes." Her cakes may not have been very beautiful, but they certainly were delicious. They suited her, too. A little rough in a charming way and sweet as could be. She'd always sit around laughing with someone. She'd bring her own chair and a little cooler box with her each time. I remember I once asked her what she kept in that cooler and she answered loudly, "Mais that's my White Mule, chere!" (White Mule was a kind of moonshine in her day.) Well, cheers in Tante Myrt's memory, because she sure was a fun person. This was my favourite thing she made.

FOR THE TOPPING

130G (3/4 CUP) DARK BROWN SUGAR

115G (1/2 CUP) BUTTER

430G (15OZ) TIN PINEAPPLE SLICES

FOR THE CAKE

335G (2 1/4 CUPS) PLAIN FLOUR

3/4 TSP BAKING POWDER

6 TBSP GROUND ALMONDS

1/2 TSP SALT

390G (1 3/4 CUPS) SUGAR

225G (1 CUP) BUTTER

3/4 TSP VANILLA EXTRACT

4 EGGS

180ML (3/4 CUP) SOUR CREAM

25CM DEEP-SIDED CAKE TIN, PREFERABLY NON-STICK.

First make the topping. Melt the butter in a pan and add the brown sugar, stirring until it dissolves and caramelises.

Pour the caramel into your greased cake tin and arrange the pineapple slices on top. Set aside while you make the cake.

Sift the flour, baking powder, almonds and salt together in a bowl. In another large mixing bowl, cream together the sugar and butter using a hand mixer. Add the vanilla extract. Mix in the eggs, one at a time, then fold in half of the dry ingredients. Add half the sour cream and mix well. Fold in the remaining dry ingredients, then the rest of the sour cream, and mix until fully combined.

Pour the cake batter over the pineapple in the cake tin and bake for about an hour or until a toothpick inserted into the centre comes out clean. Let the cake cool for 15 minutes before turning it out onto a serving dish.

DESSERTS

Gâteau de Sirop (Syrup Cake)

SERVES 10

This is a very old-fashioned recipe that Cajun ladies used to make to bring to their friends when visiting. My dad used to grow sugar cane and he'd cut and peel pieces of the cane for us to chew on as an afternoon snack. When he was younger, one of his favourite treats was getting to sample the "cane beer" made during the process of making the cane syrup. As the cane boiled, the foam and chuff that rose to the top was removed to a pot beside the fire. In the heat the sugar would ferment, and that would be used to make the beer. I'm gonna get around to trying that some day.

260G (1 1/2 CUPS) BROWN SUGAR
125ML (1/2 CUP) VEGETABLE OIL
350G (1 CUP) DARK CANE SYRUP OR BLACK TREACLE
1 TSP CIDER VINEGAR
2 TSP BICARBONATE OF SODA
1 TSP CINNAMON
1/2 TSP VANILLA EXTRACT
2 TSP GINGER
3 TBSP COCOA POWDER
1 TSP LEMON ZEST, GRATED
2 EGGS
375G (2 1/2 CUPS) PLAIN FLOUR
200G (1 CUP) RAISINS OR CHOPPED DRIED FIGS
100G (2/3 CUP) CHOPPED PECANS OR WALNUTS

23 X 33CM CAKE TIN

Preheat the oven to 180°C (350°F). Grease and flour your cake tin, then line it with greaseproof paper.

Mix the brown sugar, oil, and cane syrup or treacle in a large bowl. Put the vinegar and bicarbonate of soda in a cup with 250ml (1 cup) of very hot, but not boiling, water then pour it into the syrup mixture. Add the cinnamon, vanilla, ginger, cocoa powder and lemon zest and stir until combined. Beat in the eggs, one by one, then gradually fold in the flour, then the raisins, and then the nuts.

Pour the batter into the prepared cake tin and bake it for about 50–60 minutes or until a toothpick inserted into the middle comes out clean.

N.B. Sometimes, instead of mixing the pecans into the butter, I like to candy them in butter, sugar and cinnamon, then chop them roughly and sprinkle over the baked cake.

DESSERTS

King Cake

SERVES 10

Mardi Gras means very different things to Louisianians depending on which part of the state they were raised in. To me, Mardi Gras is multi-coloured homemade costumes, wire masks, horses, rides through the country on a trailer with live music, and a big gumbo at night. The New Orleans' Mardi Gras, on the other hand, is extravagant floats, feathered or glittery masks, brass bands, beads and doubloons, and kings and queens. It's a similar affair throughout northern Louisiana and, sadly, much of the prairie heart of Louisiana has picked up the beads, beauty pageants, and purple (justice), green (faith), and gold (power) colours in place of our own traditional celebrations.

In 2006 my brother Joel started a traditional Mardi Gras from his house (which used to be Pops' and is still called that). He and our childhood friends, Linzay Young and Lucious Fontenot, focus on keeping the Courir de Mardi Gras as traditional as possible: people are asked to make their costumes themselves and to wear wire masks and the traditional capuchons, then they ride around the area asking families to donate a live chicken, some sausage or some rice in exchange for dances and songs from the costumed participants. After the run, which is usually 5 or 6 miles, everyone returns to Pops' to slaughter and clean the chickens, make a big gumbo, and dance to live bands playing on the porch all night long.

The King Cake is actually a New Orleans tradition that came over from France and has been picked up by all of Louisiana. While Cajuns do not generally hold the same significance over the cake, we do love sweet things, and this one is really very good. The recipe here is for the traditional King Cake, but it is often filled with Bavarian cream or even chocolate.

In France, the King Cake will have different trinkets inserted into it after baking: a four-leaf clover for luck, a star for fame, or even a coin for fortune. Bakeries in New Orleans often have a special coin with their logo inserted into their cakes, but the most common prize to be found in Louisiana King Cakes is a tiny plastic baby used to symbolise Jesus. You can insert different charms to represent whatever you want to offer your family and friends, or, for a more rural cake, simple insert a whole pecan or almond into the bottom of the cake. Whoever gets the charm in their slice has either luck for the year or has to supply next year's King Cake, depending on how you want to do it. There are so many variations in this tradition that you can easily make it your own.

DESSERTS

FOR THE CAKE

- 60G (4 TBSP) BUTTER
- 90ML (GENEROUS 1/3 CUP) MILK
- 7G (1 PACKAGE) DRIED YEAST
- 450G (3 CUPS) PLAIN FLOUR
- 110G (1/2 CUP) CASTER SUGAR
- 1/2 TSP NUTMEG
- 1/4 TSP SALT
- 1 EGG & 1 EGG WHITE

FOR THE FILLING

- 115G (1/2 CUP) WHITE GRANULATED SUGAR
- 45G (1/2 CUP) SOFT BROWN SUGAR
- 1 TSP CINNAMON
- 1/2 TSP NUTMEG
- 75G (1/2 CUP) PECANS, FINELY CHOPPED
- 100G (1/2 CUP) RAISINS
- 30G (2 TBSP) BUTTER, MELTED

GLAZE

- 250G (2 CUPS) ICING SUGAR
- 1/4 TSP ALMOND EXTRACT
- 1/2 TSP VANILLA EXTRACT
- 1/2 TBSP CINNAMON
- SMALL PINCH OF SALT

In a small pan, melt the butter in the milk and then leave it to cool to room temperature.

Mix the yeast into 60ml (¼ cup) of warm water.

Put the flour, sugar, nutmeg and salt into a large bowl. When the yeast mixture has started to froth, pour it in, along with the milk/butter mixture and the egg. Mix well with your hands until you've got a rough dough, then tip it onto a floured work surface. Knead the dough, adding more flour if it's too sticky, until it becomes smooth and elastic (10 minutes or so). Butter a large bowl and put the dough in it to prove, covered with a clean tea towel.

Mix all of the filling ingredients apart from the melted butter together in a bowl.

When the dough has doubled in size (30-40 minutes), punch it down and roll it out on a floured work surface to a large rectangle about 5mm thick. Brush the surface with melted butter and sprinkle the top half of the rectangle with a thinnish layer of the filling mixture.

To make the traditional plaited ring, pick up the bottom edge of the dough and fold it over the filling. Roll it lightly, then cut it lengthwise into 3 strips. Pinch the edges of the strips if you need to stop the filling from falling out. Using a bit of water, join the 3 strips at the top and braid them loosely, pulling with your hands to stretch the strips. Use water to join the strips at the other end, then form the braid into a loop and stick both ends together. Put the cake on a sheet of baking paper on a baking tray and leave it to rise, covered with a clean teatowel, until it has doubled in size (about an hour).

Preheat the oven to 180°C (350°F). Whisk the egg white with a tablespoon of water, and brush this over the risen cake. Bake the cake for 25 minutes or until it's golden brown, then let it cool on a wire rack for 30 minutes.

Now make the icing: put the icing sugar and salt in a large mixing bowl and, using a hand mixer at low speed, slowly pour in 50ml (3½ tbsp) water. Add the almond and vanilla extracts and the cinnamon and keep mixing until the glaze is smooth and creamy. Drizzle this over the cake, leave it to set, and then sprinkle with coloured sugar – this is very easy to make at home by mixing a small bit of food colouring with white granulated sugar. Traditionally, purple, green, and gold sugar is used in sections on the cake (as a child I always wanted only the purple pieces).

If you're using charms or a plastic baby, gently lift the cake and make a small incision with a sharp knife halfway into the cake from the bottom. Insert the charm and coerce the cake back around it to close.

Notes:

While cinnamon, sugar, and raisins make up the most traditional filling, there are many options. Feel free to experiment according to your owns tastes. Some other fillings I've used and enjoyed were Nutella (I just piped a thick cord of it across each strip of dough before folding them closed and braiding) and a mix of cream cheese, egg, rum, brown sugar and cinnamon.

Alternatively, you can make a very simple royal icing using one egg white and about 125g (1 cup) of icing sugar, with a bit of lemon juice or vanilla mixed in. Glaze the cake with the white royal icing, then decorate it with coloured sugar, or you could make purple, green and gold icing and use that. Just a note if you want to do it this way—let the white icing dry before adding a colour, then let each colour dry before you add another. Otherwise they all run together and ruin the effect.

DESSERTS

Bourbon Bread Pudding

SERVES 8-10

Okay, so here is my confession. I am not a fan of bread pudding. I know I should hang my head in shame and never admit it, since it really is the most popular dessert in Louisiana, but I've got something about textures and, while bread pudding tastes delicious, I just don't like the way it feels. Anyway, I know that I have to include it for you if this cookbook is to be a fair representation of Louisiana food, and I have served this recipe to many friends who have begged for more.

Note: I normally up the bourbon in the sauce, which has made this my husband Manolo's favourite and has made our friend Russ exclaim, "It's really very good, Sarah, but I'm afraid I'll fall over if I eat another serving." If you're serving this to children, you will probably want to nix the alcohol and try a different sauce. Bread pudding is delicious with pure cane syrup, maple syrup or honey, or you can top it with fruit syrups, or crème anglaise. A dear friend, the great dancer and excellent Louisiana chef Pat Mould, once served a white chocolate sauce on a bread pudding at a cooking demonstration and it was to die for. I've used his recipe before and went a little farther and topped the finished bread pudding with the tiniest dollop of strawberry preserves.

FOR THE BREAD PUDDING:

- 100G (1/2 CUP) RAISINS
- 60ML (1/4 CUP) BOURBON WHISKEY
- 60ML (1/4 CUP) STRONG BLACK COFFEE
- 250G (9OZ) DAY-OLD FRENCH BREAD
- 960ML (JUST UNDER 4 CUPS) MILK
- 3 EGGS
- 400G (1 3/4 CUPS) GRANULATED SUGAR
- 50G (3 HEAPED TBSP) BROWN SUGAR
- 2 TBSP VANILLA EXTRACT
- 1/4 TSP ALLSPICE
- 1/4 TSP CINNAMON
- 60G (4 TBSP) BUTTER, MELTED

FOR THE SAUCE

- 115G (1/2 CUP) BUTTER
- 175G (3/4 CUP) GRANULATED SUGAR
- 50G (3 HEAPED TBSP) BROWN SUGAR
- 1 EGG
- 100ML (SCANT 1/2 CUP) BOURBON
- 100ML (SCANT 1/2 CUP) COFFEE LIQUEUR
- 3 TBSP DOUBLE CREAM

23 X 33CM BAKING DISH

The day before you want to eat, put the raisins in a small bowl and cover with the bourbon and black coffee. Leave overnight.

The next day, preheat the oven to 180°C (350°F). Cut the bread into 2cm cubes and put them in a large bowl. Pour over the milk and leave to soak until all the milk is absorbed (about 3-5 minutes). Mix once or twice to ensure that all the bread cubes get soaked.

In another large bowl, beat together the eggs, sugars, vanilla extract and spices. Add a tablespoon of the melted butter, then pour the eggy mixture into the milk-soaked bread. Gently stir in the drained raisins (if you like bourbon, you can always throw in any remaining soaking liquid as well).

Brush the bottom and sides of your ovenproof baking dish with the remaining melted butter. Pour in the bread mixture. Bake the pudding for approximately 45 minutes or until the edges begin to brown and it is firm to touch.

Meanwhile, make the sauce. Melt the butter over low heat in a medium saucepan. Off the heat, whisk in the white and brown sugars and the egg. Put the pan back on a low heat and cook, stirring continuously with a wooden spoon, until the custard thickens and coats the back of the spoon. Whisk in the bourbon and coffee liqueur, then remove the pan from the heat and leave the sauce to cool for 10 minutes. Whisk in the cream and leave for 5 more minutes. Whisk the sauce again before serving.

When the bread pudding is baked, let it cool for 5 minutes or so before cutting it into squares and serving in deep saucers with the sauce poured over.

DESSERTS

Pecan Crêpes

SERVES 4

I'm proud of this recipe. I've never had pecans served in a way I didn't love them, and I missed them in when I lived in Russia. Once, and only once, in the land of **blini** *I found a vacuum-pack of pecans and decided to try something new.*

FOR THE CREPES

150G (1 CUP) PLAIN FLOUR
2 EGGS
125ML (1/2 CUP) MILK
1/4 TSP SALT
30G (2 TBSP) BUTTER, MELTED

FOR THE FILLING

110G BUTTER (1/2 CUP) BUTTER
150G (2/3 CUP) SUGAR
150G (1 CUP) PECANS, CHOPPED
3 TBSP COGNAC OR BRANDY
125ML (1/2 CUP) CREME FRAICHE

FOR THE TOPPING

15G (1 TBSP) BUTTER, MELTED
75G (1/2 CUP) WHOLE PECANS

ICING SUGAR TO SERVE

23 X 33CM BAKING DISH

First, make the crêpes.

In a large bowl, whisk together the flour and eggs. Gradually add the milk and 125ml (½ cup) water, whisking to combine. Add the salt and melted butter and whisk the batter until it's smooth.

Heat a lightly greased, non-stick frying pan or griddle over medium-high heat. Pour 1/3 of a ladle of batter onto the hot pan, then swirl it around so it evenly coats the bottom. Cook each crêpe for 1–2 minutes on both sides, and pile them up on a plate.

Once all the crêpes are cooked, prepare the filling. Melt the butter in a pan over medium heat and add the sugar. Keep stirring and when the sugar melts and begins to caramelise, put in the pecans. Cook until the pecans are lightly browned and remove from heat. Stir in the cognac and the crème fraîche.

Preheat the oven to 180°C (350°F). Fill each crêpe with about 1–1½ tablespoons of the pecan filling and roll it up. Arrange the crêpes seam-side down in a single layer in your greased baking dish and bake them for 15 minutes.

While they bake, make your topping. Melt the butter in a small pan, and then stir in the whole pecans and any filling mixture you have left over.

Remove the crêpes from the oven and pour the hot topping over them. Dust them with icing sugar to serve.

DESSERTS

Candied Sweet Potatoes

SERVES 6

Serve them with vanilla ice cream for dessert, or next to baked turkey as a side dish!

- 900G (2LB) SWEET POTATOES
- 75G (5 TBSP) BUTTER
- 2 TBSP WHITE SUGAR
- 3 TBSP BROWN SUGAR
- PINCH OF NUTMEG
- PINCH OF CINNAMON
- PINCH OF ALLSPICE
- 3 TBSP CANE SYRUP, MOLASSES OR TREACLE
- MARSHMALLOWS (OPTIONAL)

Preheat the oven to 200°C (400°F).

Peel the sweet potatoes and cut them into 3cm cubes. Put them in a large heavy pot with 60ml (¼ cup) of water, the butter, the white and brown sugars, and the spices. Bring to the boil, then reduce the heat to low and simmer, covered, for 30 minutes or until potatoes are tender and the mixture begins to thicken slightly.

Transfer the contents of the pot to a casserole dish. Drizzle the potatoes with the cane syrup, molasses or treacle, and bake them for 40 minutes.

Note: Many Cajuns love to top these with marshmallows before baking them. I'm not a fan of the dish that way, but it is an option.

DESSERTS

Bananas Foster

SERVES 4

Okay, this is a very elegant dish – totally New Orleans and really delicious. Most New Orleans locals eat it by itself, but I love it with vanilla ice cream, the way the tourists eat it. Try it both ways and see what works for you.

- 4 LARGE, RIPE BANANAS
- 110G (1/2 CUP) BUTTER
- 175G (1 CUP) BROWN SUGAR
- 1/4 TSP VANILLA EXTRACT
- 2 TBSP BANANA LIQUEUR
- 6 TBSP DARK RUM
- 1 PINCH OF NUTMEG
- 1 TSP GROUND CINNAMON

Peel the bananas and slice them in half lengthwise, then across to quarter them.

Melt the butter in a heavy frying pan over medium-low heat, and then stir in the brown sugar. Keep stirring as the sugar melts, until it starts to caramelise.

Add the banana liqueur to the caramel, and then the bananas. Cook gently until the bananas soften and start to brown (about 3 minutes). Gently heat the rum in a small pan.

Transfer the bananas and caramel sauce to a serving dish. At the table, carefully light the hot rum in its pan and pour it, while still flaming, over the bananas. Swirl the dish to keep the flame burning and sprinkle on the cinnamon, a few pinches at a time. Keep the flames going to cook the bananas for about 2 minutes. They will die out by themselves.

Serve immediately, over ice cream if you prefer.

DESSERTS

Mom Mabel's Fig Drop Cookies

MAKES ABOUT 35 COOKIES

Our family home where my parents still live has a fig tree in a far corner of the yard, near the big garden where Dad used to grow corn, asparagus, sunflowers, and many other summer treats. I don't know if there was one on Pops' property, but I do remember the little peach tree right outside the back door that gave us loads of honey-sweet Ruston peaches every summer and the Sweet Magnolia tree by the garage that produced little flowers that smelled a little like bananas. Mom Mabel always told me to put them under my pillow for sweet dreams and I did.

You can make your own stewed figs by cooking 350g (¾lb) fresh figs, washed & chopped, with 2 tablespoons of sugar in 2 tablespoons or so of water. If you only have dried figs, use the same quantities but leave them overnight in water to plump up first.

- 115G (1/2 CUP) BUTTER
- 170G (3/4 CUP) WHITE GRANULATED SUGAR
- 1 EGG, LIGHTLY BEATEN
- 120ML (1/2 CUP) PURE CANE SYRUP OR TREACLE
- 1 TSP BICARBONATE OF SODA
- 1/2 TSP GROUND GINGER
- 1/2 TSP GROUND CINNAMON
- 1/2 TSP VANILLA EXTRACT
- 1/4 TSP ALMOND EXTRACT
- 225G (1 1/2 CUPS) PLAIN FLOUR
- 250ML (1 CUP) STEWED FIGS
- 50G (1/3 CUP) PECANS, TOASTED AND ROUGHLY CHOPPED

Preheat the oven to 165°C (320°F).

In a large bowl, cream the butter and sugar together. Slowly add the beating egg, stirring all the time, then mix in the cane syrup or treacle, bicarbonate of soda, ginger, cinnamon, vanilla extract and almond extract. Fold in the flour, and then the figs and pecans. With your hands, mix until thoroughly combined.

The dough will be heavy and sticky. At this point you can store it for up to 3 days in the refrigerator, covered tightly in clingfilm.

Break off ping-pong ball-sized pieces of dough and flatten them slightly between your palms. Place them, well spaced, on a greased baking tray and bake for 12–14 minutes or until they're golden brown. Leave the cookies to cool on a wire rack.

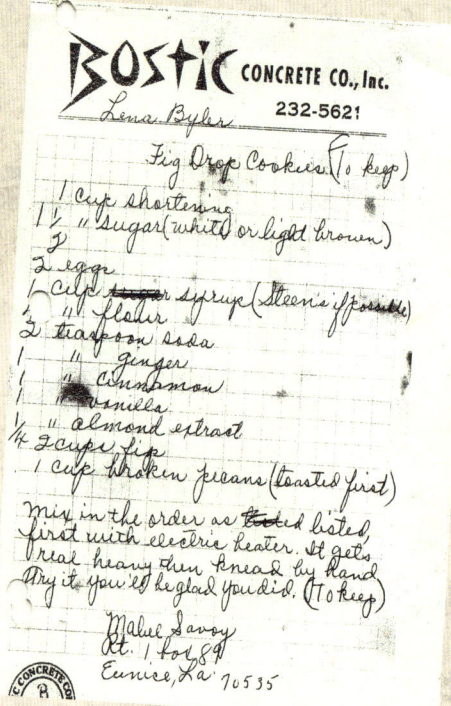

DESSERTS

Oreilles de Cochons (Pig's Ears)

MAKES 12

60G (1/4 CUP) BUTTER, MELTED

2 LARGE EGGS, LIGHTLY BEATEN

240G (1 1/2 HEAPED CUPS) PLAIN FLOUR

PINCH OF SALT

250ML (1 CUP) CANE SYRUP OR TREACLE

150G (1 CUP) PECANS, CHOPPED

VEGETABLE OIL FOR DEEP-FRYING

Combine the melted butter and eggs in a large mixing bowl. Stir in the flour and salt and mix with a wooden spoon until you have a rough dough. Turn the dough out onto a floured work surface and knead until it's smooth, then tear off golf ball-sized pieces and roll them out into thin rounds about 5mm thick.

Heat about 5cm of oil in a pan until it's hot but not smoking.

To make the twist in the dough that forms the "ear", place the tines of a fork at the centre of each round, just piercing the dough, and twist the fork a quarter turn. Drop the twists into the hot oil using the fork. Fry them, no more than 3 at a time, for about 3 minutes or until they're crisp and golden. Drain them on layered paper towels and leave to cool.

Heat the syrup or treacle in a small saucepan over medium-low heat for about 5 minutes, until it begins to thicken. Dip an outer edge of each twist in the syrup, then into the chopped nuts, and set it aside on greaseproof paper to dry.

Note: you could also use crumbled cookies, or chopped up candies instead of the pecans – use your imagination!

DESSERTS

Pecan Pralines

MAKES ABOUT 36

My Aunt Tulie (my dad's sister, Juanita Ardoin) makes these every Christmas and sneaks me a box, saying, "Hide these just for you, baby." Tulie sent me her special recipe to share with y'all.

Pralines must be the most famous southern candy and it's easy to understand why once you've tried them. They're also blessedly easy to make, so multiply this recipe by your number of friends, mix up a huge batch, pack them up in cookie tins (or plastic bags or pretty boxes), and give them as gifts at holiday parties.

```
300G (2 CUPS) PECANS
450G (2 CUPS) WHITE SUGAR
175G (1 CUP) LIGHT BROWN SUGAR
60G (4 TBSP) BUTTER
397G (14OZ) TIN OF SWEETENED,
CONDENSED MILK
2 TSP VANILLA EXTRACT
```

Turn the oven to 180°C (350°F). Put the pecans on a baking tray and toast them in the oven while it's heating up. Chop them roughly.

Fill your sink with cold water, and set a cup of cold water by your stove.

Put the white and brown sugars, butter and condensed milk in a large pan over high heat. As soon as the mixture begins to simmer, reduce the heat to medium-low. Simmer for 5–7 minutes, stirring constantly. Towards the end of the cooking time, drop a teaspoonful of the mixture into the cup of cold water: it's ready when it forms a soft ball. If you have a sugar thermometer, you want it to hit the soft ball stage (118°C or 235°F).

Remove the pot from the heat and put it in the sink of cold water. Stir in the chopped pecans and vanilla extract and keep stirring until the sides of the pot become sugary. Drop soup spoons of the mixture, well spaced out, onto greaseproof paper and leave them to set.

If the pralines don't set quickly, use a spatula to transfer them back to the pot and cook a little longer. If the mixture starts to set in the pot, return it to the stove, let it melt, and then, in Tulie's words, "hurry like hell to pour the rest!"

DESSERTS

Boules Rouges

MAKES ABOUT 20 BALLS

I'm over obsessing about whether or not to include this recipe in a cookbook about Cajun food. Boule Rouge is sickly sweet, but that's the way most Cajuns like their desserts. Even for those of us who prefer less sugary sweets, Boule Rouge represents a piece of our childhood. My grandmother and great-grandmother used to make these for my dad when he was a kid. My great aunt made them for my dad and his kids when we were little. So when we remember these people, we remember things like apricot nectar served in a Sesame Street cup, the stuffed quail and fringed lamp that sat on the table near my little rocker at my grandmother's house, which was always cool and dark and smelled like fresh meat cooking in a black pot, and… Boule Rouge. No matter how much we've all convinced ourselves that we do not like overly-sweet desserts, I dare any Cajun to try to walk past a plate of these without popping one into his or her mouth. Ain't gonna happen!

160G (2 CUPS) DESICCATED COCONUT
397G (14OZ) TIN OF SWEETENED CONDENSED MILK
1 PACKAGE RED JELL-O OR JELLY CRYSTALS

Mix together the coconut and condensed milk in a bowl, and then refrigerate it for at least an hour or until mixture is firm enough to roll into balls.

Using your hands, roll the mixture into balls about 5cm in diameter. Roll the balls in the jelly crystals so they're completely covered, and then refrigerate them again for at least an hour. You can serve them from the plate or in mini-muffin papers.

DESSERTS

Index

INDEX

A *Agnes' Biscuits* — 20

alligator
    swamp kebabs — 85

Ann Savoy
    baked beans — 49
    New Orleans-style daube — 78
    Southern-style coleslaw — 42

Atchafalaya Special Fried Fish with Crayfish Etouffee Topping — 104

aubergine
    Aubergine Pirogue — 101
    Mini Aubergine Pirogue — 35

B *Baked Beans* — 49

Baked Sweet Potatoes — 53

Bananas Foster — 131

Banana Nut Cake — 122

Barbecue — 84

Barbecue Crabs — 32

Barbecue Prawns — 31

Barbecue Sauce — 84

beans
    baked — 49
    green, zydeco — 54
    navy, soup — 68
    red, and rice — 77

Beer Batter — 112

Beignets — 19

biscuits
    Agnes' — 20
    flaky — 21

bisque
    crab and sweet potato — 66
    crayfish — 64

Boudin — 28

Boudin Balls — 29

Boules Rouges — 135

Bourbon Bread Pudding — 128

burritos
    breakfast, Cajun-style — 25

Buttermilk Pie — 119

C cabbage
    salad, Pops' — 42
    smothered — 46

Cajun-Style Breakfast Burritos — 25

cake
    banana nut — 122
    king — 126
    pineapple upside-down cake — 124
    syrup — 125

Candied Sweet Potatoes — 130

Chicken and Sausage Gumbo — 59

Chicken and Sausage Sauce Piquante — 75

Chicken Fricassee — 86

chicken
    barbecue — 85
    drunk — 85
    fried — 87
    jambalaya — 76
    wings, hot — 34

coleslaw
    southern-style — 42

cookies
    fig drop — 132

Corn Maque Choux — 43

cornbread
    Mexican — 47
    seafood — 48

Couche-Couche — 18

courtbouillon
    seafood — 91

Crab and Sweet Potato Bisque — 66

Crab Cakes Savoy — 108

Crab-stuffed Jalapeños — 37

crab
    barbecue — 32
    maque choux — 43

Crayfish Balls — 30

Crayfish Bisque — 64

Crayfish Enchiladas — 106

Crayfish Etouffee — 102

Crayfish Fettuccine — 107

Crayfish Omelette — 23

Crayfish Pie — 105

Crayfish Salad — 41

crayfish
    breakfast burritos — 25
    etouffee, Marc Savoy's — 102
    etouffee, Uncle Coonie's — 103
    etouffee, special fried fish with — 104

	Creole Chicken Fricassee	86
	Creole Stuffed Tomatoes	45
	Creole-Style Pickle Meat	77
	creole	
	prawn	90
	crêpes	
	pecan	129
D	daube	
	New Orleans-style	78
	Dirty Rice	51
	dressing	
	oyster	52
	rice	51
	Drunk Chicken	85
	duck	
	breast, stuffed	81
E	enchiladas	
	crayfish	106
	etouffee	
	crayfish, Marc Savoy's	102
	crayfish, special fried fish with	104
	crayfish, Uncle Coonie's	103
F	*Fig Drop Cookies*	132
	Flaky Biscuits	21
	Fried Chicken	87
G	*Gâteau de Sirop*	125
	green beans	
	zydeco	54
	Green Gumbo	62
	gumbo	
	chicken and sausage	59
	green	62
	prawn and okra	61
	seafood	60
	Gravy	72
H	*Hot Wings*	34
I		
J	jalapeños	
	Crab-stuffed	37
	Jambalaya	76
K	kebabs	
	swamp	85
	vegetable	85
	King Cake	126

L		
M	maque choux	
	corn	43
	crabmeat	43
	Marc Savoy	
	crayfish etouffee	102
	interview	92
	seafood medley courtbouillon	91
	Meat Pie	80
	Meatball Stew	79
	Mexican Cornbread	47
	Mini Aubergine Pirogue	35
	Mom Mabel	
	banana nut cake	122
	fig drop cookies	132
	mushroom	
	seafood stuffed	33
N	*Navy Bean Soup*	68
	New Orleans-style Daube	78
O	okra	
	gumbo, prawn and	61
	smothered	44
	omelette	
	crayfish	23
	Onion Pie	50
	Oreilles de Cochons	133
	Oyster Dressing	52
	Oysters Rockefeller	110
	Oysters Savoy	111
P	*Pain Perdue*	22
	pancakes	
	pecan crêpes	129
	sweet potato	24
	Pastry	116
	Pecan Crêpes	129
	Pecan Pie	117
	Pecan Pralines	134
	pickle meat	77
	Pickled Onions	77
	Pigs Ears	133

INDEX

pie
- buttermilk — 119
- crayfish — 105
- meat — 80
- onion — 50
- pecan — 117
- rhubarb — 120
- sweet potato — 118

Pineapple Upside-Down Cake — 124

PoBoys — 112

Pops'
- barbecue sauce — 84
- cabbage salad — 42

pork chops
- barbecue — 85

Pot Roast — 72

Potato Grenades — 55

Potato Salad — 40

pralines
- pecan — 134

Prawn Creole — 90

Prawn Dip — 36

Prawn and Okra Gumbo — 61

prawns
- barbecue — 31

Q

R *Rabbit Sauce Piquante* — 73

rabbit
- smoked, sauce piquante — 74

Red Beans and Rice — 77

Rhubarb Pie — 120

ribs
- barbecue — 85

Rice Dressing — 51

Roux — 58

S salad
- cabbage, pops' — 42
- coleslaw — 42
- crayfish — 41
- potato — 40
- spinach — 41

sauce piquante
- chicken and sausage — 75
- rabbit — 73
- smoked rabbit — 74

sausage
- Boudin — 28
- gumbo, chicken and — 59
- jambalaya — 76
- sauce piquante, chicken and — 75

Seafood Cornbread — 48

Seafood Gumbo — 60

Seafood Medley Courtbouillon — 91

Seafood Stuffed Mushrooms — 33

Smoked Rabbit Sauce Piquante — 74

Smothered Cabbage — 46

Smothered Okra — 44

soup
- navy bean — 68
- turtle — 67

Southern-Style Coleslaw — 42

Spinach Salad — 41

steak
- barbecue — 85

stew
- meatball — 79

Stuffed Duck Breast — 81

Swamp Kebabs — 85

Sweet Potato Pancakes — 24

Sweet Potato Pie — 118

sweet potato
- baked — 53
- candied — 130

T *Tasso* — 14

tomatoes
- stuffed, creole — 45

Turtle Soup — 67

U

V vegetables
- barbecue — 85

W

X

Y

Z *Zydeco Green Beans* — 54

INDEX

Notes

Notes

About the author

Sarah Savoy is a singer, musician, songwriter, cook, event planner, web designer, wife, and mother. The eldest daughter of one of Louisiana's most influential families in Cajun music and culture, Sarah left home at the age of 23 to explore the world. During a five year stint in Russia, learning the language and working as the Marketing Director of American Medical Centres in Moscow, she started playing Cajun music with friends in France and eventually decided to move to Paris to see where the band would lead her. She has now performed hundreds of concerts, festivals, cooking demonstrations and conferences around the world; released three CDs and a cooking DVD; and written this cookbook.

Find out more about Sarah and her many different projects at **www.sarahsavoy.com**